The JOURNEY to BUFFALO FEATHER

This is a remarkable Native American adventure story that will impart sacred ceremonies and rituals, accelerating your spiritual growth

---

WILLIE C. HOOKS

Copyright © 2024 Willie C. Hooks.

All rights reserved. No part of this book may be reproduced, stored, or transmitted by any means—whether auditory, graphic, mechanical, or electronic—without written permission of both publisher and author, except in the case of brief excerpts used in critical articles and reviews. Unauthorized reproduction of any part of this work is illegal and is punishable by law.

ISBN: 979-8-89419-194-2 (sc)
ISBN: 979-8-89419-195-9 (hc)
ISBN: 979-8-89419-196-6 (e)

Because of the dynamic nature of the Internet, any web addresses or links contained in this book may have changed since publication and may no longer be valid. The views expressed in this work are solely those of the author and do not necessarily reflect the views of the publisher, and the publisher hereby disclaims any responsibility for them.

One Galleria Blvd., Suite 1900, Metairie, LA 70001
(504) 702-6708

DEDICATION

"This book is dedicated to the Native American people, whose contributions and teachings have profoundly influenced my personal growth and development.

These stories aim to honor and pay tribute to the rich heritage of Native American culture. However, in order to truly understand their wisdom, I encourage you to seek direct guidance from Native American organizations, as they are the true experts. One such organization is White Buffalo, led by my dear friend Don Coyhis, who will eagerly share practical Native American teachings that can enrich your own life.

Please contact Don Coyhis the founder of White Bison at whitebison.org

I apologize in advance for any aspects that may not perfectly align with Native American teachings, as my intention is to share insights from various cultures to assist you on your spiritual journey."

CONTENTS

Introduction ix

Chapter 1   A Man Called Canyon 1

A Man Called Canyon" is a tale about Willie, an African American Brother's spontaneous journey to Napa Valley, guided by an inner impulse. He encounters an enigmatic man named Canyon a Native American at a winery and delivers a profound message to him. Canyon recognizes Willie as a divine messenger and invites him to witness his spiritual endeavors.

Chapter 2   Thunder Dog 16

In this tale, we meet Thunder Dog, a Native American Medicine Man who leads a sweat lodge ceremony. The ceremony involves purification and spiritual teachings that Thunder Dog and the elders share with the participants. The story concludes with Willie driving back home and encountering two doves in his kitchen, which leave behind feathers as mysterious symbols.

Chapter 3   Ceremony of the Pipe 31

This tale follows Willie as he attends the Native American Ceremony of the Pipe, a profound experience that shapes his spiritual journey. Amidst this ceremony, Thunder Dog imparts his teachings to Willie, unveiling the wisdom of the four worlds and their profound connection to Willie's divine purpose.

Chapter 4   Honoring Mother Earth 50

In this tale, Willie embarks on a vision quest, a ceremony dedicated to Mother Earth, despite his doubts and uncertainties. The vision quest entails Willie venturing deep into the forest alone, with occasional visits from Thunder Dog guiding him along the way.

Chapter 5   Power of the Feather 69

In this tale, Willie, Canyon, and Thunder Dog gather to discuss their plans for dealing with Crazy Deer. Willie and Canyon share their newfound powers and their readiness to confront the situation.

Chapter 6   The Sacred Union 82

In this tale, Buffalo Feather meets Mourning Dove and Naomi, a medicine woman, as they prepare the marriage costume to be worn in the Ceremony of the Pipe.

Chapter 7   A Deeper Sleep 96

This tale revolves around Thunder Dog's vision for the world, his purpose, and his eventual passing. As Buffalo Feather embarks on his journey, he discovers a serene spot beneath the night sky where he can find solace and rest, guided by his new teacher.

Chapter 8   Dancing Moon 119

In this tale, Buffalo Feather finds himself grappling with deep sorrow and depression following Thunder Dog's passing. Sensing his struggle, Naomi calls upon him to join the village for a transformative black sweat ceremony. Through this sacred ritual, she intends to help him overcome his depression, allowing him to re-engage fully in his medicine training.

Chapter 9   Spirit Keepers 136

In this tale, Buffalo Feather takes on the role of a mentor as he imparts knowledge to Dancing Moon about her native powers. He enlightens her about the profound abilities she possesses as the Four Spirit Keepers are bestowed upon her, each aligned with a specific direction.

Chapter 10 Butterfly Clan 149

In this tale, Dancing Moon discovers that she possesses the extraordinary powers of the Butterfly Clan and wields the element of air. Symbolizing transformation and influence, butterflies become her embodiment as she becomes a formidable force of change and inspiration.

Chapter 11 Skeleton Spirit 164

In this captivating tale, Naomi takes charge of a skeleton spirit sweat by adorning hot stones with the aromatic sweet grass, creating a mesmerizing incandescent aura. As she begins to sing, a mystical gathering unfolds, where peculiar entities materialize, including a greenish skeleton adorned with feline-like teeth, accompanied by five diminutive skeletons.

Chapter 12 Cardova 170

In this tale Buffalo Feather awakens abruptly in the dead of night, a palpable sense of a presence permeating the room. With a mix of curiosity and trepidation, he diligently searches every corner, but his efforts yield no evidence of anything out of the ordinary. Yet, the unsettling feeling of being watched continues to persist, casting an eerie shadow over his surroundings.

Chapter 13 The Student is Ready 198

In the concluding tale, Buffalo Feather immerses himself in the realm of creation, he undergoes a remarkable and profound shift within his being. A renewed sense of purpose takes hold, firmly planting its roots within him, while a profound connection with the enigmatic mysteries of the universe blossoms.

As we venture through these stories, we will unravel the rich tapestry of spirituality, interconnectedness, and the timeless wisdom of ancient traditions. So, let us embark on this extraordinary odyssey, where magic and profound truths await us at every turn.

INTRODUCTION

Welcome to an enchanting journey through a collection of mystical and captivating tales. In the Journey to Buffalo Feather, we will explore twelve intriguing stories filled with spirituality, ancient Native American traditions, and the interconnectedness of all living things. Each narrative invites us to delve into the realms of mysticism and discover the profound wisdom hidden within their pages. From the ethereal dance of a Native American Medicine Man named Thunder Dog, to the sacred ceremonies honoring Mother Earth, these tales will transport us to a realm where the spiritual and natural worlds intertwine. Join us as we embark on this extraordinary adventure, where the boundaries between reality and the supernatural blur, and the power of the human spirit unfolds.

Chapter 1

A MAN CALLED CANYON

I lay motionless in my bed, basking in the warm morning sunlight that permeated my soul. The sunbeams caressed my bare body, infusing me with a sense of life and freedom.

As I absorbed the healing sunlight, my body grew stronger, invigorated by its nourishing rays. My spirit melded with the light, embracing a sense of unity. Along with this unity came a powerful urge to head north. With a renewed sense of vitality, I got up and made my way to the bathroom, indulging in a rejuvenating shower. The warm water cascaded over me, offering a gentle massage, as my mind wandered to distant places. I envisioned myself standing beneath a magnificent waterfall on a paradise island. Eventually, the daydream concluded, and I stepped out of the shower, drying myself off and getting dressed. It was time to embark on my journey.

I hopped into my red Nissan and set off. As I stopped at a traffic light, I turned northward. A sign on my right read, "Entering Interstate 280 north, the world's most beautiful freeway." I couldn't help but acknowledge the truth in that statement. The rolling hills, adorned with lush green grass, embraced the road on both sides. The land exuded positive energy, teeming with animal life. To my right, two deer and a rabbit peacefully grazed, basking in the morning sun. Overhead, a hawk and an eagle soared, their majestic flight in search of sustenance. On my left, a stunning reservoir stretched alongside the freeway, its tranquil waters inviting seagulls to dive for food. It was undeniably shaping up to be a remarkable day.

Continuing my northward journey on Interstate 280, I eventually reached the Highway 1 turnoff and proceeded further north. A sign caught my attention, indicating the right lane for the Golden Gate Bridge. I signaled and merged into the right lane, embarking on a route that would lead me through San Francisco and onto US 101, ultimately crossing the iconic Golden Gate Bridge. The water beneath the bridge glistened invitingly, while a fleet of proud U.S. Navy ships floated beneath, including an aircraft carrier and several other impressive vessels. Boats adorned with vibrant sails added to the scenic spectacle. As I reached the other side, I glimpsed at the majestic bridge in my rear-view mirror, its grandeur etched in my memory.

My destination remained uncertain until a sign appeared, announcing, "Napa Valley exit 10 miles." In that moment, a voice whispered in my head, urging me to take that exit and venture into Napa. Trusting my instincts, I turned onto Highway 29, and before long, sprawling vineyards unfolded on either side of the road, painting a picturesque landscape.

Passing one vineyard after another, a compelling impulse compelled me to stop at a particular winery. I hesitated for a moment, questioning if this was truly the reason for my journey to Napa Valley. Yet, the feeling persisted, prompting me to make a U-turn and return to the winery.

The sign above the entrance revealed the name "DeMoor Vineyard." I cautiously pulled into the parking lot, finding a spot near the entrance. Moments later, I walked through the doorway, and a voice behind the counter greeted me, "Hi, welcome to DeMoor Vineyards. My name is Jasmine. Come on in and taste our wonderful wines."

Engaged in conversation with Jasmine about the wines, my attention was diverted by the entrance of a peculiar man. He sported cowboy boots, a long-sleeved shirt, and blue jeans, while his hair was tied back with sinew and flowers. Adorning his neck was an extraordinary necklace, adorned with colorful beads and unfamiliar stones, including a prominent eagle's claw. The necklace emanated a strong spiritual energy.

Unexpectedly, this enigmatic man began shouting words that were unintelligible to me, directed at an unknown recipient. It was evident that he was agitated and angry about something. Despite my initial surprise, words seemed to flow from within me as I felt compelled to address him.

"A brave warrior must exhibit patience and control over his anger to succeed in battle. Anger, as you know, is merely a manifestation of fear, and fear must be conquered before one can truly become a great warrior," I uttered. The expression on his face revealed surprise, matching my own.

Curiously, he asked, "Who sent you here?"

I said, "I am just a man, much like yourself—perhaps not as courageous. A strong inner impulse guided me to drive north this morning, leading me to this winery and to you. Although there is a message for you, I do not comprehend its meaning. I only know the words I have spoken to you, and I cannot explain their significance," I replied.

Canyon, as he introduced himself, appeared taken aback. "How did you know that I am a sacred pipe carrier?"

"The how and why of this day remain a mystery to me. All I know is that I am here in this moment," I responded.

In that instant, an instinctive gesture led me to reach into my pocket, discovering an object I had no recollection of placing there. As I retrieved the item, I was astonished to find it was a copy of "Daily Affirmations from the Divine Creator." This book contained affirmations I had written to share the wisdom and richness of Native American culture.

Canyon's eyes gleamed as he beheld the Medicine Wheel depicted on the book's cover. "This book must be intended for you," I said, extending it towards him. "I wrote it several years ago to assist individuals in harnessing the profound wisdom of the Native American culture."

Canyon accepted the book from my hand, closing his eyes in what appeared to be a silent prayer. When he opened his eyes, he embraced me warmly. "You are a messenger from the Divine Creator. Wait here for just a moment." He walked outside, ascending a grassy hill and dropping to his knees. Holding the copy of "Daily Affirmations from the Divine Creator" overhead, he moved it ceremoniously from right to left and back. When the book reached eye level, he opened it, meticulously examining its contents, his face radiating with joy.

Inside the winery, Jasmine and I stood in silence, unsure of how to proceed. We patiently waited for Canyon to complete his ritual. After a few minutes, he rose from his kneeling position and returned to the winery.

"Will you come to the mountain where I reside and witness what I am constructing?" he asked. "Together, we can find clarity by burning sage."

A thought flashed through my mind—the world would be a better place if we treated each other as the sun treats us. The sun shines upon all individuals equally, without discrimination based on the color of their skin—red, black, yellow, or white. The sun's unconditional love provides a profound lesson for humanity. Sunshine, bestowed upon us freely by Father Sky, is a wondrous gift, demanding nothing in return. As the thought faded, I realized Canyon was awaiting my response.

"Yes, Canyon, I will gladly accompany you to the mountain and witness your endeavors. I will assist in any way possible. The message you were meant to receive has already been delivered, and with time, its true meaning will become clear to you," I assured him.

"Excellent," Canyon exclaimed as he walked behind the counter, joining Jasmine. "I serve as the manager of the winery's gift shop. Hence, anything you desire today is on the house."

"I do not drink, but I would appreciate a bottle of dessert wine," I replied.

"Coming right up," Canyon responded, retrieving a case of dessert wine.

"Thank you," I expressed my gratitude.

He placed a fancy corkscrew within the case, and Canyon selected various gifts from behind the counter, adding them to the wine case. His generosity extended further as he included a few more presents. Chuckling, he said, "There you have it—a week's worth of gifts."

"Thank you once again," I expressed, uncertain of what I would do with all the items he had bestowed upon me. Yet, an inner voice advised me to accept them graciously. I smiled and thanked him once more.

The encounter at DeMoor Vineyard marked the beginning of an extraordinary journey, a convergence of fates intertwined by the whispers of the Divine Creator.

Canyon said, "I get off work at 5:00. Can you come back to the winery around then? If so, you can follow me to the mountain. The drive will take about 45 minutes."

"Yes, I can be back at 5:00. That will give me plenty of time to eat and see some of the Valley."

I bid goodbye to Jasmine, and Canyon and I walked to my car. When we reached the car, we stopped and embraced. As we held each other, Canyon said, "You are my spiritual black brother and a divine messenger. Although I must be patient, I look forward to being in your silence. Your silence is healing." He smiled and walked away.

After getting back into my car, I resumed my drive north on Highway 29. I made a stop in the little town of St. Helena and had a late lunch. Following the meal, I did some window-shopping along St. Helena's bustling main street. There were a few bookstores, clothing stores, and even a couple of antique shops to explore.

Time flew by, and before I knew it, it was 4:00. I hopped into my car and headed directly to DeMoor. When I arrived at the parking lot, Canyon was already there, standing next to an old black pickup truck. I pulled my car up close to his and rolled down my window.

"Good to see you again. This is my pickup. We should leave now if we want to be on top of the mountain when the sun sets."

"Let's go. I'll follow you," I said.

Canyon hopped into his pickup and drove south on Highway 29. I followed him closely but made sure not to tailgate. After about 10 miles, Canyon turned off Highway 29 onto a bumpy back road that led up the mountain. As we ascended the steep slope, my car's engine shifted into high gear. I could feel the pressure change in my ears as we climbed to higher elevations. Canyon increased his speed as the time for the sun to set drew nearer. At one point, I was surprised to see my speedometer reach 80 miles per hour. However, I knew my car couldn't handle much more.

After an hour of ascending the steep and winding mountain, Canyon slowed down. It seemed that we were almost there. He signaled a left turn by putting his arm out of the window. I followed suit and completed the turn, revealing about 10 small huts on the right side. The huts formed a circle amidst a group of trees. Constructed with a combination of wood and sturdy canvas, they appeared to be a blend of a house and a tent. The huts looked fragile, as if a strong gust of wind could cause them to collapse.

Canyon gave a signal, and I stopped as he parked his pickup. He walked towards me and signaled for me to drive behind him. I followed his lead, driving slowly as he guided me to the designated parking spot. Once I parked and got out of the car, Canyon said, "This is where I live. It's peaceful here. Let's go quickly, as the sun is setting."

Without exchanging a word, I followed Canyon up a small trail that led to an opening in the trees. From there, we were greeted with a breathtaking view of the valley stretching for miles. As I took in the beauty of the surroundings, I was captivated by the most exquisite sunset I had ever witnessed. Overwhelmed by the moment, I sat on the ground, closed my eyes, and savored a brief moment of tranquility. After a while, I opened my eyes and continued to immerse myself in the enchanting beauty of the forest and the sunset.

When I glanced over at Canyon, I saw him on his knees, picking up some earth in each hand. With deep respect and reverence, he held Mother Earth's precious and powerful essence in his hands. As the earth slowly sifted through his fingers and returned to the ground, he honored the Divine Creator, Father Sky, and Mother Earth for the blessings of that day. It was at that moment I became aware of my ability to sense his thoughts and emotions. For about 30 minutes, neither of us spoke a word. Both of us sat on Mother Earth's embrace, appreciating and honoring the wondrous creation of the Divine Creator.

After the sun disappeared below the horizon, Canyon and I stood, filled with joy. Breaking the silence, Canyon spoke, "I enjoy the beautiful sunset as often as possible. It always fills me with joy and love for humanity. Now, let me show you what I'm building." With that, he turned and led the way down the trail towards his hut.

Near the bottom of the trail, he veered to the left onto another path. We walked approximately 100 yards to a cleared area where Canyon was constructing a sweat lodge. He mentioned that the sweat lodge would be ready for use the following month and invited me to return to experience a purifying sweat bath, cleansing both body and mind.

"He said a sweat bath is a sacred ceremony that held great power and served as a profound ritual of purification."

A potent energy emanated from the sweat lodge. I expressed to Canyon my admiration for his work. I also promised him that someday I would return for a sweat purification in his lodge.

Canyon proceeded to explain the construction of the sweat lodge in more detail than I wanted to know. "We create the sweat lodge by planting 16 willow sticks upright in a circle. These willows are then tied together, forming a dome that stands about four to five feet high. The dome is covered with buffalo skins, tarps, and blankets. The sweat lodge can accommodate six to ten people. Inside the lodge, people crouch around a small fire pit, representing the sun, which sits in the center. The sun, as the great giver of life and energy, radiates its warmth throughout the lodge. The fire pit also serves as a vessel for the heated stones, over which cold water is poured, enveloping the participants in hot steam."

He continued his teaching, "The sweat lodge draws upon the powers of the universe, including the elements of earth, water, fire, and air. Water symbolizes the thunder beings, who bring goodness. The steam that rises from the rocks within the lodge purifies us, allowing us to live in accordance with the Divine Creator's will. If we attain a state of purity, the Divine Creator may even grant us a vision."

Canyon then shared the significance of the chosen ground for the sweat lodge. "The location we selected for the sweat lodge is near water and abundant with wood and white willow. White willow holds great power and can alleviate headaches caused by the sweat. Additionally, it is essential for the entrance of the sweat lodge to face west, uniting the setting sun and the night sun, also known as the moon."

Canyon meticulously explained all the aspects of the sweat lodge construction, as if he believed that one day, I would build my own lodge. He truly was a skilled teacher and communicator.

Chuckling, I remarked, "Canyon, you're quite the talker."

He responded with a smile, saying, "Let me show you the last Sacred Giant Sequoia Tree in this area. All the other Sequoia Trees have been cut down, but this one remains."

I agreed, saying, "Okay," and followed him as he led the way.

Canyon walked about five feet ahead of me as we ventured into the increasingly dark forest. Suddenly, he came to a halt and instructed me, "Willie, stop right there. Don't come any further until I call you."

I replied, "Okay."

Canyon proceeded towards a cluster of trees, disappearing from my sight. Though I couldn't see him, I sensed the reason for his pause. We both felt a change in the energy surrounding us, a negative and formidable presence. Uttering unfamiliar words in a chanting tone, Canyon's voice exhibited little modulation but steadily increased in volume. I caught glimpses of his body moving in a dance-like manner. While I couldn't comprehend the words he chanted, I had a distinct understanding of what was transpiring. As Canyon danced, his body at times resembled a majestic eagle and at others a powerful mountain lion. He invoked the powers of his totem animals.

Intuitively, I understood that Canyon was attempting to drive away the malevolent spirits that had blocked our path. Their strong negative energy permeated the air, quickly enveloping us. Deciding to take action, I dropped to my knees and entered a deep state of meditation. My spiritual energy surged, flowing outward to fill the space around us. As my spiritual energy continued to flow freely, a profound healing silence engulfed the environment. Although Canyon persisted in his chanting, no sound emerged from his mouth. My silence formed a protective cloak around us. The potent healing silence gradually dispelled the malevolent energy. Opening my eyes, I noticed the return of sound to Canyon's chanting. He ceased his chant and beckoned me to join him. Ascending a slight slope, I reached his side. No words were necessary. We both understood the events that had transpired and the danger we had encountered.

As we proceeded on our way towards the Sacred Sequoia Tree, a large bear suddenly emerged, startling both of us. Luckily, the massive creature wandered off into a dense wooded area and down the slope, showing no interest in us. We burst into laughter, relieved by the bear's lack of concern.

Canyon remarked, "I'm glad it was just a bear. I've had enough encounters with evil spirits for one night. It took both our spiritual powers to ward them off."

Finally, we reached our destination—the most colossal Sequoia tree I had ever laid eyes upon. Standing before me, mouth agape and heart wide open, I found it hard to believe what I was witnessing. The tree's branches were the size of smaller trees, while its trunk resembled a small house. Despite its enormous size, it exuded beauty. The wisdom, love, and spiritual energy emanating from the Sequoia Tree were almost overwhelming.

As I circled around the sacred Sequoia Tree, I paused and embraced it with both arms.

As we made our way back to his hut, I shared with Canyon the experience of embracing the sacred Sequoia Tree. Upon our arrival, I noticed an animal cage outside the door.

Curious, I asked, "Can I see what's inside?"

Canyon responded, "You can look inside the cage, but you mustn't touch the baby fox inside, whose mother was killed. It will stay with me until it can be reintroduced to the forest. If the baby fox becomes too accustomed to humans at such a young age, it will lose its ability to survive in the wilderness."

Canyon opened the cage, and I peered inside. There, I beheld a cuddly little baby fox. It resembled a puppy and exuded playfulness. The fox's fur was long and black, with pure white tips. Curious, I inquired, "Why does the fox's fur have white tips?"

Canyon explained, "When this fox was born, its fur was entirely white. As it grew, its rich white coat gradually turned black, starting from the fur closest to its body. What we see now represents the last remnants of white that this fox will ever have as a cub. Native people believe that when someone witnesses the final disappearance of the white fur on a baby fox, that person has been chosen to share in the fox's potent medicine and will receive the wisdom of the fox to guide them on their earthly journey. It is also a spiritual sign that the individual is on the pathway of the Divine Creator."

He turned to face me and continued, "I have never witnessed the complete transition from white to black fur in a baby fox, so I cannot tell you what occurs. However, I have overheard others speak of the experience, and they have described it as truly spiritual and insightful. As a young boy, I often stayed awake throughout the night, waiting, watching, and hoping to witness the transformation. Regrettably, I was never successful. Back then, I felt disappointed and saddened because I could not witness the baby fox's metamorphosis. Yet, over the years, I have come to understand that the Divine Creator did not intend for me to possess all the powers within fox medicine. Instead, the Divine Creator has bestowed upon me numerous other wonderful and powerful spiritual medicines to aid me on my journey."

"What are the spiritual powers of the fox?" I inquired.

Canyon replied, "The sacred powers of the fox grant you the marvelous ability to vanish and remain unseen by others. You can also merge with your surroundings and become an observer of people and situations. As a masterful observer, you can create a clean space for others to bring forth their special divine gifts. Being detached from them and the situation, you can maintain a spiritually clean and nurturing environment. Detachment liberates you from hate, jealousy, desire, anger, and fear. The divine gift of detachment enables you to perceive the past, present, and future as one. Sacred fox medicine encompasses numerous special powers, and I have already witnessed and felt some of these powers within you."

Canyon recognized that he needed to tap into the power of the fox to become more cunning in his dealings with the Napa Valley City Council. He believed this to be the only way to reclaim the bones of his people and provide them a sacred burial place. I smiled and remarked, "Canyon, I see that you are embracing the message of patience in your quest for returning the native bones. Like the fox, you possess the ability to adapt to change."

"Let's enter my hut and burn some sage," he suggested.

His hut consisted of two small and well-organized rooms. The left room served as a bedroom, adorned with a buffalo skin-covered bed. We stood in the slightly larger room, which functioned as a combined living room and kitchen. The kitchen area housed a small stove for cooking and heating purposes, along with a sink providing running water. I didn't spot an indoor bathroom, so I assumed it was located outside.

Neatly arranged books adorned both rooms, while two pictures graced the canvas walls. On the west wall, a depiction of an ancient Native American man wearing a war bonnet caught my attention. The other picture hung above the dresser, depicting Canyon and a woman around his age, sitting on a black pickup truck in the desert, embracing each other.

Combat ribbons and other military items were scattered around the room, indicating Canyon's past military service. A large hunting knife with a sharp cutting blade and a bone handle rested on a table.

A grandiose grandfather chair and a small couch occupied one side of the living room. Canyon gestured for me to take a seat on the couch, and I obliged.

"You have a lovely place," I complimented.

"It's my home, and it has everything I need. Plus, it's peaceful and quiet. I have two of the huts in this village—this one and the one to the left. If you ever feel the desire to reconnect with nature, give me a call at the winery, and this place is yours. You're welcome to return anytime. If I'm not here, I'll likely be camping in these woods. Help yourself to anything you need. I've informed all the families in the camp about you. Jasmine resides just three huts to the right. She will remember you. She already refers to you as my brother with divine messages."

"Thank you for your kind invitation," I expressed my gratitude.

Canyon settled into the big grandfather chair and retrieved a bag of sage. He pulled out a sage leaf, lit one corner, and handed it to me. I accepted the sage with my left hand. He procured another leaf and ignited the corner, holding the burning sage in his left hand. I realized that I must be doing everything correctly since I mirrored his actions precisely. As the smoke billowed from the burning sage, Canyon drew the smoke toward his body with his hand. Slowly, he moved his right hand up the left side of his body, approaching his head. When his hand reached about two inches above his head, he gradually directed it to his right side, tracing down the right side of his body with his hand. Surprisingly, the smoke followed his hand's path.

The sight of the smoke descending along his body surprised me. In my experience, smoke was meant to ascend, not descend. He repeated the tracing motion along the same trajectory.

When he withdrew his hand from the smoke, it continued to flow in a counterclockwise circle along the path he had traced. Canyon's closed eyes and distant expression indicated his deep meditation. Intrigued, I decided to follow the same process. As I traced my body with my right hand, the smoke obediently followed, forming a counterclockwise circle around the upper part of my body. Even after removing my hand, the smoke continued to flow in the same manner as Canyon's had. As the smoke gracefully circled, my mind became filled with numerous thoughts, immersing me in a dreamlike state.

Suddenly, the urge to use the bathroom disrupted my reverie. Opening my eyes, I heard Canyon say, "Welcome back."

"I feel like I've been on a long journey. Now I really need to use the bathroom," I chuckled.

"The bathroom is outside near your car," he informed me. "Let me fetch two items you may need." Canyon opened a storage drawer and retrieved a flashlight and some toilet paper—Charmin Ultra Soft, to be exact. I couldn't help but burst into laughter. It seemed amusing that a man living in his manner would opt for such squeezable soft toilet paper. Smiling, I accepted the flashlight and toilet paper from him without uttering a word.

With the darkness enveloping the surroundings, I switched on the flashlight. The baby fox inside the cage was scratching, catching my attention. Opening the cage cover, I met the playful gaze of the fox. Locking eyes with it, I observed the transformation taking place within its fur. The fox frolicked under the light as the beam danced inside the cage. Suddenly, the white tips of its fur turned black.

Curiosity piqued, I moved the light closer to my side of the cage, hoping the fox would follow and allow me a better look at its black fur. As anticipated, the fox followed the light and drew near to where I stood. Its fur had now completely turned black, save for a white spot about the size of my hand on its back. Intrigued by the remaining white fur, I noticed it formed the shape of a small turtle. Within moments, the white, turtle-shaped fur vanished, leaving the fox entirely black.

Overwhelmed with excitement, I hurriedly returned to the hut and relayed the remarkable transformation to Canyon. He shared, "You have witnessed the sacred transformation of the fox. The fox has chosen to bestow upon you its powerful spiritual medicine. The turtle on the fox's back signifies that you will possess both fox and turtle medicine to guide you on your journey."

Canyon and I engaged in hours of discussion about spiritual powers and their utilization to fulfill our divine purposes. Before we realized it, the sun began to rise. Recognizing that it was time for me to depart, I assured Canyon that I would wield my newfound fox spiritual powers responsibly. We bid each other farewell. As I drove down the mountain, my mind was filled with the enchanting occurrences of the past few hours.

Upon reaching home, I parked my car in the driveway and prepared to exit. To my surprise, a beautiful eagle feather lay on the passenger seat. I couldn't recall seeing the feather during my drive home from Napa Valley, yet there it was—a gift, undoubtedly from Canyon. He had mentioned possessing powerful eagle medicine.

In my heart, I sensed that one day in the near future, I would return to visit the man named Canyon.

Chapter 2

THUNDER DOG

Over the past 6 months, I had returned to the Native American village in Napa many times to continue my training with Thunder Dog. Then, one evening at around 8:00, I pulled my car into the driveway. It had been a long day. Although I felt too tired to get out of the car, somehow, I managed. Inside, I walked upstairs to the bathroom. In a hurry to relax, I started the hot water running into my Jacuzzi bathtub. I undressed quickly as I was anxious to get into the soothing water, but the big tub was filling very slowly. In my mind, I could already feel the warm water flowing all over my body.

When the tub was completely full of soothing hot water, I stepped gingerly into it one foot at a time. Unfortunately, I had not given my body the necessary time to adjust to the extreme temperature change and soon felt a little light-headed. Gradually, I immersed myself in the water and turned on the air jets. In my haste to get into the tub, I had forgotten to put my favorite raspberry bubble foam into the running water. Overcoming my resistance, I jumped out of the tub and got the bottle of bubble foam. Since I was already out of the tub, I ran downstairs and got a can of cold Pepsi to drink during the bath. It wasn't long before raspberry bubbles filled the tub and their wonderful aroma scented the air. The water was still quite hot as I slumped down to allow the air jets to blow on my back and neck. It was heavenly to relax there in the tub with water flowing all over me.

The tranquilizing water took me into deeper and deeper levels of relaxation. Soon, I felt as though I did not have a care in the world. While lying there, I thought about Canyon. I felt that he wanted to talk to me. I tried to dismiss the feeling, but it persisted for about five minutes. After a short interval, all feelings and thoughts of Canyon left as suddenly as they had come.

After about 45 minutes in the bath, my skin had become wrinkled from the hot water, so I got out and dried myself off with a big bath towel. The sound of the big tub draining filled the air. It was about 10:00 p.m., and I was sleepy, so I tumbled into bed. Soon, numbness moved over my mind, and I slept.

I was fast asleep when a large eagle appeared and circled about my body. Its spiritual powers and great wisdom were flowing out to me. A bolt of lightning frightened me as it lit up the room with a flash of bright colors. Although I tried as hard as I could, movement was impossible. The giant eagle grew larger and larger as it circled freely about me. I tried to speak but could make no sound. Apparently, the eagle did not intend to harm me. Breathing deeply, I told myself everything would be all right. It was then that the eagle spoke. It said, "I can hardly wait to be in your silence again."

Suddenly, I knew that the eagle was Canyon, but I still could not move toward him or speak with him. Just as quickly as the eagle had come, it was gone. My body lurched out of the bed with a force that awakened me from deep sleep. A glance at the clock showed that it was 2:00 a.m.

My mind pondered the dream as I lay in bed, hoping to drift back to sleep. After a while, my mind grew hazy, and sleep overtook me. Again, I was awakened, this time to a tickling sensation on my forehead. It felt like the tiny legs of a little bug dancing on my face. I quickly brushed my forehead with my hand and opened my eyes. To my surprise, it was not a bug but the feather of an eagle. Surely, this had to be a message from Canyon. He had the medicine powers of the eagle to guide him on his journey, and he had used them to communicate with me. There was no feeling of him being in any danger. Even so, I was anxious to call him at the winery, but it was too early.

I was completely awake, so I got out of bed filled with a sense of focus and purpose for the day. It was my intention to go to the mountain to visit Canyon.

It was 9:00 a.m. by the time I was up and dressed. I picked up the phone and called DeMoor Winery. The man who answered told me that Canyon and Jasmine no longer worked there. They had quit the winery to participate in a three-month-long celebration honoring the lives lost at Wounded Knee. I thanked him for his information and hung up the phone. I decided to go to the mountain anyway.

I got into my car and laid the eagle's feather on the passenger seat. It was my feeling that Canyon wanted me to bring the feather along. I felt some very strong spiritual power emanating from it, and it was alive with great medicine and healing energy.

As I started the car's engine and began my drive to Napa Valley, many unexpected and exciting memories of my prior visit returned in a flash of emotion, sights, and sounds. I reflected on the beauty of that drive and the invisible force that guided my direction. This trip was much like my last drive to Napa Valley, but then I had not known the purpose of the journey. Although unsure of what this expedition might hold, I felt better prepared for my new adventure. The spirit of the mountain was calling me.

After about forty-five minutes of driving north on 280, I turned onto US 101. A short time later, I made another turn onto Highway 29, which took me into the valley. The memory of which road to take to get to Canyon's mountain was hazy, but I was determined to find it. Driving slowly north, I looked carefully at every road that crossed the highway. Because I was driving so slowly, many impatient drivers behind me frantically honked their horns, but I just smiled and kept looking for my turnoff.

I searched my memory diligently, but none of the side roads seemed to match the picture in my mind from my previous trip. I was running out of options, so I pulled over to the right shoulder and stopped. The feather brushed my hand, and immediately a big hit of Canyon's spiritual energy permeated me. The feather was guiding me and told me that this was the right place. I pulled the car back onto the highway, entered the left lane, and turned left at the next crossroad. Although the landscape did not look familiar, it felt correct. The strain on the car told me that I was starting up a steep grade. I pressed harder on the accelerator, and the speed increased. The eagle's feather disappeared from the dashboard right before my eyes. A thorough search of the car revealed the feather was nowhere to be found. It was gone.

A close look at the scenery showed nothing familiar, but I felt this was the correct path, even if it was not the same road. A voice from within the car said, "Trust your intuition. Let your spiritual powers guide you to the village. We are waiting to be in your silence, my great brother with divine messages." I smiled and then laughed out loud, accelerating to 65. The steep grade was straining the car's engine.

When the top of the mountain was in sight, I slowed the car to a crawl. Canyon was standing on the left, waving his arms and signaling me where to park. I parked where he indicated and got out. He met me with a big hug.

"We have been waiting for you. The medicine man and the elders are here. We are almost ready to start our sweat. Thunder Dog, the medicine man, is inside the sweat lodge purifying it before we enter. He insisted that you join the sweat," he said.

"It's good to see you again," I said. "Although I'm unsure of why you wanted me to come to the mountain. Here I am. I wasn't sure if I could find my way back to the village. All the way up the mountain, it didn't look like the same road that we used the last time."

"It isn't the same road that we used," Canyon said. "The north road that we took is closed for repairs. That's why the feather guided you up the mountain using the south road."

"I wondered what the feather was for. You sent it to me to use as a homing beacon. Is that why you took the feather away when I got on the right road?" I asked.

Canyon said, "No. I didn't want to take it away at all, but Thunder Dog, the medicine man, wanted the feather taken away. Thunder Dog knew you didn't need the feather. He said your powers of insight and vision were strong, therefore you didn't need any help to find the village. Thunder Dog is waiting to lead us in a sweat. He knew that you gave me many powerful messages that helped me recover the native bones from the Napa Valley City Council. He has visited you many times over the past few months in your dreams and visions. He knows that you need the power of a sweat to bring out more of your spiritual powers and to get your native medicine flowing. He does not want you to lose your way on your journey. You'll understand it all when you meet Thunder Dog in the sweat. He has invited three of the elders to join us. You have just enough time to prepare yourself."

Canyon and I walked to the sweat lodge where he introduced me to the three elders. Their names were Lame Deer, Black Fish, and Little Turtle. They were old and appeared to be very wise, although they did not say much. They were also naked and waiting to enter the sweat lodge.

"We must bathe in the waterfall before entering the sweat lodge," Canyon said. "The waterfall is just a few yards away."

I didn't remember seeing a waterfall the last time I was there, but Canyon talked about it. In my mind's eye, I visualized standing under a beautiful waterfall with its purifying waters flowing over the mountain before falling a hundred feet onto my body. I had never taken a bath under a waterfall before, and I was excited.

Canyon and I undressed and took a short walk. The waterfall was not as I had expected. It wasn't big at all. It looked as if someone was standing on top of the mountain with a water hose regulating the amount of water to fall on each of us. The water fell on me after I had stepped into the pool of water. Much to my surprise, it was ice-cold. It occurred to me that maybe I wasn't ready for this outdoor life. Just a few hours ago, I was taking a shower in hot soapy water, and it had felt wonderful. Now, I was standing naked in freezing cold water in the forest. Although I tried not to think about how cold the water was, it did not help. On the contrary, the more I wanted the water to warm up, the colder it got.

Thunder Dog's voice entered my mind. "This waterfall is like life: the more you resist what is, the more it persists. You must accept what is and extend your love to all, regardless of the situation. Do not live life resisting what is. It is much easier to ride a horse in the direction that it is going."

Canyon said, "I know the water is cold to you, but resisting it will not help. You must accept what is in order to live in harmony and in love with all. Thunder Dog is ready for us to return to the sweat lodge."

We got out of the waterfall and dried ourselves off with towels that were lying on the rocks. We each wrapped ourselves in a buffalo skin that Jasmine brought.

"Hi, are you going to join the sweat?" I said to her.

"No, it's my moon time. I'll take a sweat another day with some of the other women. It's good to see you, black brother with divine messages. I noticed you didn't like the cold water. The next time, remember that the water is only cold for those that resist it. Have a great sweat, and maybe I'll see you later, and you can tell me all about it." She turned and walked away without saying a word to Canyon.

Canyon and I walked over to the sweat lodge. Thunder Dog signaled that the sweat lodge was holy, and we should enter. Canyon and I removed our buffalo skins and joined the elders. The sweat lodge was very low, and we got down on all fours to enter. Once inside, I felt the sage-covered floor underneath my hands and feet. Thunder Dog was sitting at the east side of the sweat lodge.

When we were all seated, Thunder Dog's helper started passing hot rocks in from outside the sweat lodge. It seemed as if the helper had passed in thirty hot rocks before Thunder Dog signaled him to stop. With each rock, the lodge got hotter. Thunder Dog sprinkled sweet grass and a dipper of water over the glowing rocks. Its fragrance quickly filled the sweat lodge. Thunder Dog said that the sweet grass would prevent us from getting headaches as a result of the hot steam coming off the rocks.

The others waved the steam toward them as it rose from the hot rocks. They rubbed it over their faces and chests. I watched and then did the same.

Thunder Dog started singing a prayer song. Canyon and the elders quickly joined in. I was not sure what the song was, but before long, I was also singing the words. It was as if I had recalled this song from some forgotten place deep in my mind or soul.

Though I felt clean and refreshed by the purifying steam, the sweat lodge was becoming uncomfortably hot, as I was not accustomed to the heat. The hot steam curled around my back and caused a large blister on my right shoulder.

As the air moved over, around, and across the fire-filled rocks, it felt too hot to take in. I quickly cupped my hands over my nose and mouth, hoping to cool the hot air before inhaling it. Canyon and the elders smiled. It occurred to me that I must have looked funny trying to cool hot air with my hands.

The fire pit in the center of the hut represented the sun. It was the real source of the heat. The air was hot, and I was trying to keep from crying out for the flap to be lifted, but I could not. The heat was so intense that I cried out, "Hot." Then the entrance flap was lifted, and the cool air from outside rushed into the lodge. The outside air was welcomed with open arms. The flap would have been lifted four times during the ceremony, even if no one asked for it, but I could not wait for the first lifting. After a few moments of relief, the flap was once again closed, and the flow of cool air was cut off. The hot steamy air immediately started filling the sweat lodge. This time, it seemed to be a little easier for me to inhale as the steam invaded my lungs.

Thunder Dog noticed that I was able to handle the hot air better, so he resumed praying. Thunder Dog told me to meditate. During the meditation, I quickly slipped into a place of deep oneness with the Divine Creator. Powerful spiritual energy was flowing in the sweat lodge and within my mind, my heart, my body, and my soul. Big drops of sweat formed and fell from my body. A drop of sweat formed on my chest and turned into a big, hairy monster. The monster dropped from my body and lay on the floor. It grew bigger and uglier and more terrifying. I could not believe my eyes, but there it was. The monster sprang up and disappeared through the sweat lodge wall.

Thunder Dog's said, "Do not be concerned. It's just fear coming out of you and leaving this holy place." I felt as if I should be afraid, but somehow, I wasn't.

I watched as another drop of sweat formed on my body and slowly transformed into yet another monster. It also grew bigger, uglier and more terrifying before disappearing through the sweat lodge wall. Again, Thunder Dog's voice boomed, "That was your anger coming out and leaving this holy place."

As I watched, resentment, jealousy, greed, hatred and other negative feelings and emotions came from my body as drops of sweat. Each drop of sweat turned into a hideous monster and vanished from the sweat lodge. After a few minutes, I felt clean, refreshed and purified by the Divine Creator's spiritual energy. As I rubbed myself dry with sage, a great feeling of friendship and unity with Canyon, Thunder Dog, and the Elders consumed me.

Canyon had the copy of *Messages from the Divine Creator* that I had given him. He opened the book and read aloud from it. Canyon recited many affirmations before he stopped and closed his eyes. His eyes remained closed for just a moment. When he opened his eyes, he said, "You are my brother and we have great work to do.

Canyon continued by saying, "Many of my people have gone to the spirit world, but we can still catch glimpses of their wisdom and thoughts in the sweat lodge. I love all that has been created. I love every living human being on this earth and in the universe. I love every plant, every animal, from the largest tree to the smallest flower, and from the great mountain lion to the tiniest bug. I have a very intimate relationship with the Earth, the wind, and all animals."

When I looked at him again, the book had disappeared and Canyon's eyes were open. He smiled and I felt him honoring Thunder Dog, the Elders and me.

Thunder Dog's voice broke the silence. "Now we are purified and we can begin our orange smoke." He signaled that the entrance flap be lifted. He took the sacred red stone pipe from the altar and lit the grains of tobacco in its bowl with a red-hot buffalo chip.

Thunder Dog began the sacred ceremony by taking a draw on the sacred pipe. He said, "All things are interrelated. Everything in the universe is a part of a single whole. Everything is connected in some way to everything else. We can understand anything if we understand how it is connected to everything else."

Thunder Dog passed the sacred pipe clockwise to Lame Deer, who took a draw on the pipe. He began, "Change. All creation is constantly changing. Nothing stays the same, there are always cycles of change. One season follows the other. Human beings are born, live their lives, die and enter the spirit world. All things change. There are two kinds of change. The coming together of things is called development, and the coming apart of things, is called disintegration. Both kinds of change are necessary and are always connected to each other."

"Changes happen in cycles or patterns. They are not accidental or without purpose. Sometimes it is hard to see how a particular change is connected to everything else. This usually means that our ability to see is limited by our situation."

Lame Deer passed the sacred pipe clockwise to Black Fish, who took his draw on the sacred pipe. He began to speak. "The seen and the unseen. The physical world is real. The spiritual world is real. Yet, separate laws govern each of them. When we break the spiritual laws, it can affect the physical world. When we break the physical laws, it can affect the spiritual world. A balanced life is one that honors the laws of both the physical world and the spiritual world. Human beings are spiritual as well as physical."

"Human beings can always acquire a new mind, a new body and new spiritual gifts. The timid person may become courageous. The weak person may become bold and strong. The insensitive person may learn to care for the feelings of others. The person who values only money and material things can begin to look inside and listen to his inner voice. When human beings develop new qualities, this process is called development, or true learning."

"There are four parts to every person's nature - physical, mental, emotional and spiritual. These four parts are developed through the use of our free will. A person cannot learn in a totally whole and balanced way unless all four parts of his being are involved in the learning process."

Black Fish passed the sacred pipe clockwise to Little Turtle, who took a long, powerful draw on it. He said, "We must develop the spiritual aspects of our nature. We have the capacity to respond to nonphysical realities like dreams, visions, ideas, spiritual teachings, goals, and thoughts. We have the capacity to understand that these nonphysical realities can teach us about our own potential to do or be something more, or different from what we are. We have it within us to express these dreams, visions, ideas, spiritual teachings, and our own goals and thoughts through our interactions with the world. We must stay actively involved while developing our spiritual energy."

"The doorway through which all must pass if they wish to become more spiritually awakened is the doorway of free will. A person must decide to take the spiritual path. The spiritual path has never-ending patience. It will always be there for those who decide to travel it."

"Anyone who sets out on a journey of spiritual development will be helped. There will be guides and teachers who will appear, and spiritual protectors who will watch over the traveler. No test will be given that the traveler does not already have the strength to meet. The only way to fail on the journey will be the traveler's own failure to follow the teachings of the Divine Creator."

Canyon received the sacred pipe from Little Turtle and took a short, smooth draw on it. He recited a silent prayer. After the prayer, Canyon said, "We can gain a vision of what our potential is from the teachings of the Divine Creator. By living up to our spiritual purpose and by living our lives according to the spiritual laws, we will grow and develop spiritually. Our spiritual purpose is like a strong magnet pulling us toward living our lives through our Higher Self."

Canyon completed his prayer and handed me the sacred pipe. When holding the pipe, I felt it continually moving. Thunder Dog was communicating with me. "While we are smoking the sacred pipe, it's alive. It is the flesh, blood, and mind of native people. That is why you feel its movement."

Great power flowed from the pipe into my veins. Smoke rose from its bowl as I took a draw. The spiritual power was increasing in the sweat lodge. Although I felt giddy from the steamy heat and lightheaded from the sacred tobacco, my body, mind, heart, and soul were purified with the Divine Creator's holy energy. Certain powers were now present. At some point, the Divine Creator's energy had filled the sweat lodge, as well as our minds, bodies, and souls.

The flap was closed, and Thunder Dog placed the sacred pipe back on the altar. Suddenly, a big eagle's feather appeared in front of me, and I was instantly transported from the sweat lodge into an open field of beautiful flowers. There were thousands of wonderful flowers. As I stood there naked in the middle of all those colorful flowers and wonderful smells, an incredible healing power flowed over my body, mind, heart, and soul.

The eagle's feather was not the same feather I had seen before. This feather was as big as a house and very powerful. This eagle's feather was for me. Somehow, I knew it had belonged to me long ago. The feather started moving away from me, and I ran toward it, trying to keep it in sight, but it moved too fast for me to keep up with it. The feather was almost out of sight when a great black buffalo came galloping over the distant horizon towards me. The eagle's feather was attached to the buffalo's back.

Thunder Dog's spiritual presence was there, and he said, "Your native divine name is Buffalo Feather." I knew right away that what Thunder Dog said was true. It also occurred to me that I must acknowledge my native name to increase my spiritual power as I followed the path to oneness and harmony.

As the buffalo passed close to me, I quickly jumped upon its back. The buffalo never slowed, not even for a moment. When I took the feather in my hand, the buffalo, the eagle's feather, and I became one. The powers of the buffalo flowed into my veins. The powers of the great eagle flowed through the feather and into my veins. These powers felt alive and made me feel so strong that I did not know if I could handle them. Our bodies and physical form transformed into a pure ball of intense glowing light. We lifted off the ground and flew high overhead.

In my position high above the planet, I saw all the negative darkness and all the healing light in the world. As I looked upon the darkness in the world, tears came to my eyes. I wept like a child as I experienced all the sadness in the collective heart of mankind. As my tears ran down my face, they fell upon the darkness on the planet. These fallen tears immediately created powerful spiritual light that surrounded and healed the darkness.

A voice from within me said, "Buffalo Feather, it is your purpose to bring your powerful spiritual gift forward to help heal the negative darkness that is in the world. You must live your life from Higher Self and be an example of my spiritual laws in action as you journey along your worldly existence. Extend your spiritual love to everyone in the human family. The symbolic races - red, yellow, white, and black - are all part of the same human family. They are all brothers and sisters living on Mother Earth. They are all part of me, and no one is separated from me."

I heard my voice say, "Yes, I will fulfill my divine purpose."

Suddenly the ball of light that I was part of disappeared along with the feather and the buffalo. I found myself back inside the sweat lodge.

Thunder Dog said aloud, "Welcome, Buffalo Feather, you are now a great medicine man in training. You also have many spiritual powers to share on your journey." Then everyone in the sweat lodge started chanting "Buffalo Feather, Buffalo Feather," repeatedly.

My eyes filled with tears as a wonderfully loving feeling flowed over my mind and within my heart. I was deeply honored to be in a sweat with my brothers.

Thunder Dog signaled that the flap be raised and that the sweat was complete. I knew that Thunder Dog, the elders and Canyon had held the sweat to teach me their ways and to help me reaffirm my divine purpose. As we exited the sweat lodge one by one, I thought to myself that my new brothers had done a wonderful job. It felt great to stand up and stretch my legs. As I looked up at the stars and the universe, I thanked the Divine Creator for all his wonderful gifts.

Although it was after midnight, I was feeling so good that I decided to drive home. As I said good-bye to Thunder Dog and the elders, each of them called me Buffalo Feather and we embraced. The name made me feel centered.

After we dressed, Canyon and I walked to my car. Canyon asked if I wanted to stay over until morning.

"No, I just want to be in silence and relive the rich experiences of this entire day."

Canyon nodded. "I understand. I want to do the same thing myself. I received my own divine messages and need to reflect on them."

"Say good-bye to Jasmine for me," I said, "and thank her again for the towels and the buffalo skins at the waterfall."

He had a strange look on his face. Canyon started to say something, but changed his mind and remained silent. We embraced and I got into my car and drove away.

Soon I was home parked in my garage. There was no eagle's feather lying on the passenger's seat this time. I got out of the car and went inside the house.

Two beautiful doves lit on the counter in the kitchen. They danced in a loving ceremonial fashion before they disappeared. Each left one of its powerful feathers before disappearing through the kitchen ceiling. I picked up the lovely feathers and wondered what they meant.

Chapter 3

CEREMONY OF THE PIPE

As it had been a slow day at work, I decided to leave early for a change. I quickly cleaned up my office and casually walked out the door around 3:00 p.m.

"I'll be at home in about an hour if anyone needs me," I said to Susan, my administrator, who sat just outside my office.

"OK. Can I leave early too?" Susan smiled.

"One of us has to mind the store, otherwise we'll both be looking for a job."

We laughed, and I walked down the hall and out the front lobby. I got into my car and drove along the side streets toward Interstate 280.

A short time later, I exited the highway at Edgewood and stopped at the sign near the end of the off-ramp. From out of nowhere, a dove landed on the hood of my car. I looked closely as it returned my gaze through the window. The dove was about 13 inches long. Its body was bluish-gray with bronze markings on its wings and a whitish rump. A few moments later, a second dove with long iridescent hackle feathers that hung down over its back and shoulders landed beside the first. The second dove danced, circling the first. Both doves made a cooing noise as they circled each other.

After a few moments, the male jumped onto the back of the female dove, and they began mating. I didn't know what to do. Should I drive off or just wait for them to finish on my hood? Should I turn off my engine? All I did was turn off my radio. I didn't know why. At some subconscious level, I must have known that the doves wouldn't enjoy mating to James Brown singing in the background.

To make things worse, the cars behind me started honking their horns. Perhaps they couldn't see what was happening on my hood. After a few minutes, they started pulling around me, continuing on their way.

By this time, the doves were mating so passionately that my car was shaking violently. I couldn't believe that two birds with such small heads and short stout bodies could create such an intense physical force. Nothing seemed to bother them. The more they mated, the louder and more magical their melodic cooing became.

The cooing put me into a trance. To break from the trance, I closed my eyes and opened them quickly. To my surprise, the faces of the doves transformed into those of Jasmine and Canyon. I couldn't believe it. Once again, I closed my eyes, and this time I opened them slowly. My friends' faces were still there. As I looked more closely, I saw the intensity of their expressions.

Suddenly, the air smelled of burning sage, and I felt a warm breeze ripple through the open window. I was more than a little concerned about the doves with human faces mating on my hood. I couldn't turn my head away from them. Their faces wore big smiles.

After a few more moments of mating, the dove on top hopped off. Then both of them danced in a loving, ceremonial fashion while cooing harmoniously. They finally flew off and disappeared into the bright sun.

A dark green Lexus pulled up next to me. The driver rolled down his window and said, "What kind of man are you that doves make love on your car? Birds only crap on my car." Then he laughed and drove off.

I looked around to ensure the doves were completely gone, then I made my right turn onto Edgewood and continued driving home. I pulled into the garage, still wondering what it all meant.

In the kitchen, there were two dove feathers lying on the counter. When I picked them up, I felt their spiritual power. Jasmine's strong energy was present within the feathers. I ran upstairs to find the feathers I had received a few months ago from the doves that had disappeared through my kitchen ceiling. Those feathers should have been in a dream catcher hanging over the bed, but they were no longer there. They had disappeared or somehow made their way downstairs to the kitchen counter.

Then I knew Thunder Dog and Jasmine were sending me a message. I sat on the side of the bed with a feather in each hand and slowly closed my eyes. Instantly, I felt myself in communication with Thunder Dog.

"Good," he said. "Buffalo Feather, it's good to see that although you walk in four different worlds, you haven't forgotten the teachings of the red one. Jasmine and Canyon have requested permission to undergo the Ceremony of the Pipe. If their request is to be honored, you must be there."

"I'll be there. But what is the Ceremony of the Pipe?" I asked.

"I won't make it so easy for you. If you haven't figured it out by the time you're here, I'll tell you. You already know, but you must look within yourself for the answer."

My communication with Thunder Dog slipped away, and I slowly opened my eyes. I put the feathers on the bed, dialed my office, and waited impatiently as it rang.

"Good afternoon. Willie Hooks' office. This is Susan. May I help you?" Susan's voice came through the line.

"Susan, what does my calendar look like for the rest of the week?"

"Home already? Let me get your calendar. You have a meeting with finance on Thursday, but I can reschedule if you like. Your customer meeting in Tulsa next week has been canceled. So next week is open."

"Do you mind if I take a vacation for the rest of this week and next week?"

"I'll fill out your vacation cards and send them in. Have a great time. Promise me you won't do any work - not even on your laptop. I think you need a break. I'll tell everyone not to call you at home either. I'll let Steve know that he'll be sitting in for you."

"Thanks, Susan. I promise, no working, and I'll see you when I get back."

After packing a few things, I was ready for my trip to the Ceremony of the Pipe. I took a shower, put on some soft music, and picked up the dove feathers. I laid in bed feeling totally relaxed.

As I lay there with a dove feather in each hand, I thought about Thunder Dog's words. I reflected on a conversation Thunder Dog and I had about the four worlds and their uniqueness. He had said, "Each of the four worlds - red, yellow, black, and white - has many different nations within it. Each nation has its own unique culture, customs, identity, and values that they feel they must defend. If you walk between nations that are trying to protect themselves from outsiders, you will not be at home in any of them."

"For example, worldwide there are about 125 different values. These values are the foundation from which communities and individuals obtain guidance. The few values selected are based on the nation's culture and the location on Mother Earth where the people live. Mother Earth is extremely diverse. Our location on her is one of the deciding factors in the values we choose. Only certain sets of values will allow us to live in harmony with certain regions on Mother Earth. Our culture and values govern our thought process, behavior, and communication. To understand people of different nations, we must honor their cultural values. Honoring the values of others does not mean that we give up our own."

"Although nations perceive reality differently, we all have the same spiritual laws at our core. Extending love, practicing forgiveness, praying, and being grateful are consistent universal principles that work all over the world. At the level of the soul, we are all spiritually connected as brothers and sisters. We are also physically connected by Mother Earth and Father Sky."

"Because you have been chosen to walk in all four worlds, you have taken on an extra burden. You'll be a stranger in each one, even the world in which you were born. At the same time, you will be a brother or sister to everyone if you stay at the level of spirit. You'll be in exile in each world because each will feel that they must protect themselves. Even so, you will always have a home because you are living from spirit and soul. You can see the paradox. The Divine Creator has placed you on this paradoxical pathway because it is part of your purpose. You are an instrument of integration and unity for all worlds and all nations. The pathway will be difficult and easy at the same time."

"Each world has a unique way of perceiving, thinking, and communicating. They have different languages, words, and symbols. A word rich with meaning in the white world may have the opposite or no meaning at all in the red, yellow, or black one. So, communicating with words can be a problem. To walk this paradoxical pathway demands a great deal of awareness. Understanding is not enough. You must be fully aware to live in harmony in four worlds. Trying to live by spiritual laws in one world is more than enough for most people. It requires a great warrior to live spiritually in four worlds."

"Even when you come to visit me, you're in exile because you are not of this nation. But at the same time, you and I were born to be brothers. Wherever you go, your purpose is not to visit, for fellowship or even to be home. Instead, you go to teach, to learn, to heal, to unify, or to cleanse. Walking in four worlds is a difficult journey."

My mind was running wild with thoughts. Thunder Dog's words helped me understand why I felt like an outsider everywhere I went, though everyone welcomed me as a friend and brother. Living this dilemma had been hard and often painful. I experienced deep emotional anguish as I reflected on these feelings of isolation.

A single tear rolled down my face. After carefully placing the feathers on the nightstand, I lay back and allowed my eyes to close. Although it lasted a long time, the sadness finally passed, and I fell asleep.

The sound of soft music from my alarm awakened me. After a few minutes, I got up and went through my morning routine, which took about an hour. Once ready, I carefully picked up the two feathers and made my way downstairs. A quick review of my preparations for the two-week absence assured me that everything was ready. I put the feathers in the passenger's seat of my car, backed out of the garage.

A few minutes later, I was on the Interstate heading for the Napa Valley. While crossing the Golden Gate Bridge, I noticed several small sailboats in the bay below. During the drive, I continued to meditate on the Ceremony of the Pipe. Holding one of the feathers, I began to repeat, "Ceremony of the Pipe," aloud. Suddenly, my thoughts were transported back to my last visit with Canyon. We had just stepped out of the waterfall, drying ourselves off with towels lying on the rocks. Jasmine had brought us two buffalo skins to wrap ourselves in. While

Jasmine and I carried on a friendly conversation, Canyon and Jasmine had never spoken a word to each other.

After my sweat, when I was getting ready to drive home, I had asked Canyon to say goodbye to Jasmine, but he had never confirmed. He also had a funny look on his face every time I mentioned Jasmine. Something seemed off between them, which didn't make sense given their strong friendship.

I picked up the other feather and held both of them in my right hand. Instantly, Canyon's energy enveloped me. As I headed for Napa, his energy grew stronger and stronger. I placed the feathers back on the seat, and Canyon began communicating with my mind.

"Hi, Buffalo Feather. I'm anxious to be in your silence again. The last time we met, I couldn't speak of Jasmine because we were in the process of deciding to get married. In our tradition, when two people are considering marriage, they don't talk to each other for months. They can't speak each other's name or even look at one another. This sacred period forces them to be separated and in silence so that their hearts and souls won't be influenced by each other's physical presence. During the ninety days, we were both encouraged to see other people and even have relationships if we wanted, but I am not interested in anyone else. The purpose of the separation is for us to do anything that will help us make the right decision. It also gives us one last chance to complete old relationships and desires to make space for our new loving journey. After that time, if we still desire to get married, we both want you to be there. I also require your help with some other issues that have developed, but I will wait until you're here to share more."

"I'm on my way. Why is it called the Ceremony of the Pipe?" I asked.

"We have requested to be married by the pipe to the Council of the Elders and Thunder Dog. When two people are united through the Ceremony of the Pipe, the union can never be undone. Any other marriage can be terminated, but ours can never end, no matter what happens. Even if one of us dies, the other can never remarry. It's a serious decision that requires the highest approval in our tribe. We don't know if our request has been accepted. I sensed Thunder Dog communicating with you. He knows I need your help, and I feel much better knowing you're on your way."

"How many ways are there to get married in your culture?" I inquired.

"There are three ways. The first type of wedding is casual, where a couple simply sets up a house together. Often, parents arrange the alliance with the help of a go-between, but there is room for romance. A person in love may persuade their parents to take the necessary steps. There is no formal exchange of vows, only a few ceremonial gifts from the man to his in-laws. Divorce is also easy, as the couple simply parts ways when the relationship has run its course. By custom, the woman always keeps both the house and children.

"The second way is more formal, with a wedding ceremony performed by a medicine man, chief, or elder. After a few prayers and spiritual vows, the couple is pronounced joined as one.

"The third is the Ceremony of the Pipe, reserved for couples who both understand and are aware of their Divine Purpose. A relationship united by the pipe is lifelong with no possibility of divorce. These unions are rare because the individuals must have reached a stage in their development that requires their combined energy to achieve their purpose. They must also convince the council of elders, medicine man, and chief that they can live up to the commitment and that their union is part of a divine plan. The medicine man must have a vision of the divine purpose of their union before he can honor their request."

"Sounds like Jasmine and you have a spiritual purpose to fulfill. You both must be honored," I commented.

"Yes, we do. I have been fasting alone in the forest for many days to test my fortitude and to feel the supportive yet challenging forces of nature. This purification process has brought forth many dreams and visions of supernatural forces that will guide and protect Jasmine and me throughout our lives," Canyon replied.

"You have a lot of powerful medicine to support you in completing the ceremony and to protect you on your journey. It will be good to see you and Jasmine. I am honored to be a part of the wedding," I expressed.

"I must go now, so that I can meet you. I have just returned from a long, hot journey," Canyon said.

"I'll be there soon." Canyon's energy disappeared, but his words echoed in my mind as I continued driving. Twenty minutes later, I arrived at the village. After parking, I walked toward Canyon's hut.

Canyon emerged from the woods to greet me, and we embraced for a long moment before slowly walking toward his hut. It felt comforting to see him and be in the red world again. The air was filled with the refreshing scent of pine trees, and a cool breeze moved through the lush green forest.

I noticed a hawk soaring high in the sky directly above us. The wind currents against its wings allowed it to hover in place. It was a magical sight to witness the black-winged hawk suspended in the sky, its head turning slowly from side to side as it began its descent.

"What is that hawk doing?" Canyon asked.

"The hawk is the messenger of the sky. It has come to bless your union. Let's sit with the hawk's energy for a while," I suggested. We knelt on the ground and closed our eyes.

In a matter of moments, the powerful energy of the hawk enveloped us. The hawk, Canyon, and I were in communication. The hawk spoke,

"Canyon, the visions you had during your fast were not mere dreams. You must learn to distinguish between the two. A vision is when all your dreams have vanished, and you no longer possess a dreaming mind. You are learning to be observant and open. As you become more alert, the Divine Creator will approach you through all your senses. Learn to observe your surroundings and acknowledge that the Divine Creator is present in everything. As you become more aware, you will one day realize that trees, flowers, and everything around you are truly manifestations of the Divine Creator. I bless you with my magical powers to guide you on your journey."

"Buffalo Feather, you are teaching Canyon the power of observation and the importance of understanding the broader vision. You are also assisting him in mastering my powerful medicine so that he can fulfill his divine purpose. You play a significant role in this wedding ceremony because your spiritual medicine will help integrate my potent hawk energy into their union. With my powers fully developed within Canyon, this relationship will remain fresh and vibrant with divine love. He will perceive the obvious in everything and recreate his love anew with every action," the hawk conveyed.

The hawk let out a mighty cry, and I felt its powerful shriek dissolve layer after layer of our unawareness. Our unawareness continued to slip away until we were left kneeling in total truth, fully present. A tingling sensation spread throughout my body. We opened our eyes and looked up just in time to see the hawk vanish into a beam of white light. The light slowly ascended until it disappeared from sight.

"The hawk has bestowed its powers upon me, and I feel blessed," Canyon declared.

"You now possess the powerful hawk medicine to guide you on your journey. Nothing can hinder Jasmine and you," I reassured him.

"You are not entirely correct on that point. I have not seen Jasmine for the past three months. I know how she feels about me, but she has many others to choose from," Canyon confessed, his voice filled with pain and cracking with emotion. We sat on the ground, legs crossed, and looked at each other. Deep emotions were evident on his face.

"Is she seeing someone else? It seems that you two have a divine purpose to fulfill," I inquired.

"Crazy Deer, the son of a chief, loves her deeply. He has always wanted Jasmine to be his wife. They lived together while I was away **in Vietnam**. When I returned, she left him and moved in with her mother. He was angry about her departure and blamed me for confusing her. It was time for him to focus on his preparations to become chief, and that training consumed him for two years. During that time, Jasmine, Crazy Deer, and I rarely saw each other. Each of us had many challenges to overcome, but I knew my love for her would never waver," Canyon explained.

"When did you and Jasmine start seeing each other again?" I asked.

"A few years ago, Jasmine and I happened to meet at the Peyote Ceremony. It was an unexpected encounter, but the moment we looked into each other's eyes, we knew that we were deeply in love. Over time, our love for each other grew stronger and stronger," Canyon shared.

"What is the Peyote Ceremony?" I inquired.

"The Peyote Ceremony is a sacred ritual that transports your spirit into the void of the universe, where there is no time or space—only raw creative energy emanating from the Divine Creator. This ceremony enhances your awareness of the power you possess to create fear or joy in everything you do. It helps you realize that you hold the power to conquer your fears by confronting them. It connects you with your pure creativity and allows you to confront your fears, ultimately embracing your true self. Embracing your true self brings great freedom into your life," Canyon described.

"The Peyote Bird, or Water Bird, is the Totem of the Peyote Ceremony. This sacred Medicine Bird observes its own reflection in the pond. The gift of self-examination enables the seeker to see the aspects of themselves that lie beneath the surface of physical reality, leading to the discovery of universal consciousness," Canyon added.

"Isn't peyote considered a drug?" I asked, seeking clarification.

"Many people believe that peyote can drive one to madness. However, the sacred manner in which we gather our plants prevents it from becoming a drug. We honor the life force of each plant and offer prayers of gratitude with each selection. We always leave an offering of tobacco for Mother Earth, expressing gratitude for the powerful medicine she has provided. Each plant is strung on a dream string and allowed to dry for an extended period behind the bed of the person who will partake in the medicine. Each peyote bud is cut with a ritual representing the Four Directions and then either powdered or made into tea. No part of any bud goes to waste. Through this sacred process, peyote becomes an integral part of the ceremony," Canyon explained.

"In the Peyote Ceremony, Jasmine and I discovered our immortal spirits and new ways to develop our abilities. We also realized that our union was necessary to fulfill a divine plan and enhance our true selves. The ceremony revealed our sacred path and guided us in overcoming our fears. Since then, our love for each other has deepened," Canyon explained.

"I'm starting to grasp the situation. The more Jasmine and you saw each other, the more upset Crazy Deer became," I commented.

"That's correct. When Jasmine informed Crazy Deer that we had requested the Ceremony of the Pipe, he became highly emotional. If it were still our tradition, he would have challenged me to a fight to the death. However, we no longer practice that custom as it does not honor a woman's right to free choice. Nevertheless, we are allowed to energetically battle for a woman's hand, and that's precisely what Crazy Deer is doing. He hopes that his energy is strong enough to drive me away and potentially win Jasmine over. My fear of losing her is so strong that I'm afraid he might be winning," Canyon admitted.

"What else has he done?" I inquired.

"Crazy Deer was so upset that he told Jasmine the ceremony would never happen. Then he vanished into the woods without any food for about four weeks. During that time, I felt his negative energy surrounding me each day. He appeared in many of my dreams, and he even turned some of them into nightmares," Canyon revealed.

"Where is he now?" I asked.

"After returning from the forest, he began courting Jasmine. He is always by her side, trying to persuade her to be his wife. He believes they are still married because they lived together for two years. I hope she is telling him that they are not married, but I'm not entirely sure. Jealousy, pain, and fear have clouded my mind to the point where I can no longer sense her energy within me. Despite my attempts to communicate with her energetically, I am unable to do so. I feel like I'm losing both her and my sanity. Crazy Deer's energy and power are so formidable that he may succeed in pulling her away from me. Perhaps Thunder Dog sensed my fear and decided to call upon you for help. He himself is not permitted to intervene with his powers. Your presence brings me a sense of balance and harmony. Just holding your image in my mind makes me feel more empowered. Buffalo Feather, I desperately need your assistance. It's a matter of life or death," Canyon pleaded.

"How can I help?" I asked.

"Let's walk further into the forest, and I'll explain more," Canyon suggested.

Evidently, he didn't feel comfortable discussing the matter in our current location. Suddenly, the wind shifted, and a peculiar odor filled the air. The atmosphere became heavy, and an irritating buzzing sound resonated in my right ear.

"Follow me quickly," Canyon urged, and we ran into the forest.

We eventually ceased running and began walking side by side, delving deeper into the forest.

"What was that?" I asked, still puzzled by the strange occurrences.

"That was Crazy Deer. He was attempting to test your energy. He is aware of your presence and suspects that you may be planning to assist me. He wanted to gauge the strength of your powers, but we moved before he could locate us," Canyon explained.

"His power was strong, and there was another energy accompanying him," I observed.

"I didn't sense anyone else besides Crazy Deer, but it was likely Black Hawk, his best friend. Black Hawk serves as the apprentice to their clan's medicine man. My awareness is so blocked that I am rendered useless," Canyon admitted.

"So, you have been engaged in a battle with Crazy Deer, the son of a chief, and Black Hawk, the apprentice to a medicine man?" I confirmed, trying to grasp the gravity of the situation.

"Yes, and now you understand why I need your help. Your spiritual powers are growing stronger each day, and as an apprentice medicine man working with Thunder Dog, you possess the potential to aid me.

I don't have much time left to end this battle, or else my soul will be lost," Canyon implored, revealing the urgency of the situation.

"Tell me about the battles with Crazy Deer and Black Hawk. What has happened?" I asked, eager to understand the nature of their encounters.

"It all started a few weeks ago. Crazy Deer's energy woke me from a deep sleep. It surrounded me and filled the entire hut. The air became pungent, and his unsettling presence lingered. I quickly rose to my feet and emanated positive energy to challenge the negative presence. For a moment, it receded. But then a second energy joined in and attacked me with such force that I was knocked to the floor. The combined forces lifted me up and threw me across the room. They were so strong that when I attempted to get up, they threw me back onto the bed. In frustration, I shouted, 'What do you want?' Suddenly, they lifted me and transported me to a place deep in the forest. When I landed, I had no idea where I was. After wandering for a few days, I managed to find my way back to the village. However, three days had passed. If this happens the day before the Ceremony of the Pipe, Jasmine and I won't be able to marry," Canyon explained, his voice trembling with emotion.

"So, Crazy Deer's strategy is to physically keep you away from the ceremony," I deduced.

"Yes, that's what I believe. A week later, while I was sitting in the forest, praying and using sage, the combined energies of Crazy Deer and Black Hawk suddenly surrounded me. They moved so swiftly that I couldn't put up much of a fight. This time, their powerful energy transported me both physically and mentally back in time to a place covered in ice. It was incredibly cold, with large glaciers slowly carving into the coastline.

Initially, I didn't know how to return to the present. It took numerous attempts, but eventually, I utilized my spiritual horse medicine to fly forward in time. It required all of my power to make my way back.

When I reached Thunder Dog, he informed me that I had been gone for two weeks. He also revealed that Crazy Deer is challenging my right to marry Jasmine by the pipe because he doesn't want her to be bound to a marriage that cannot be undone. Crazy Deer had also seen Jasmine as his wife and divine mate during a vision quest, he undertook while fasting in the forest for four weeks," Canyon recounted.

"How is that possible? How can Jasmine be his divine mate and yours simultaneously? Do you think Crazy Deer is lying about seeing Jasmine as his divine mate in his vision quest?" I asked, perplexed by the conflicting claims.

"I can't explain it. However, Crazy Deer does not lie. He is a great warrior, and one day he will be a great leader. He wouldn't deceive about something like that," Canyon insisted.

"I can't quite grasp it. Did anything else occur?" I inquired.

"Yes, one more thing. After I returned from the cold place, I found it extremely difficult to stay warm. I had to keep a fire going constantly and sit near it as often as possible. One night, while I was sitting by the fire, the energies of Crazy Deer and Black Hawk descended upon me and extinguished the flames. Immediately, I was transported forward in time to a desert region. The temperature during the day soared to 120 degrees. The sand felt like red-hot coals, and the air lacked any moisture, leaving my mouth parched. To make matters worse, the temperature dropped near freezing at night. I believe I was in the northern hemisphere, although I can't be certain. A vast mountain range stretched for miles, and the landscape was desolate, making it difficult to find food or water. It took me two weeks to find a way to employ my dragonfly magic and return to this time and place. I have only been back for three days," Canyon recounted, his voice filled with the weight of his experiences.

"When do you think they will strike again?" I inquired.

"If Crazy Deer and Black Hawk follow their pattern, they won't engage me in battle for another week or two. They always provide me with a few days between attacks to contemplate my decision. They don't want to kill me, but they will torment me with fear if they believe it necessary. Their ultimate goal is to make me leave without marrying Jasmine," Canyon explained, his fear visibly growing.

"Do you believe that our combined energy is strong enough to defeat them?" I asked, hopeful yet uncertain.

"No, not at the moment. Our current power is insufficient to overcome them. However, you are a medicine man apprentice. Thunder Dog has been teaching you how to tap into Mother Earth's power. He mentioned that Mother Earth is waiting to share many gifts with you in a special ceremony dedicated to her. As you continue to develop your newfound powers, I believe we may just have enough strength to emerge victorious," Canyon expressed, his hopes resting on the potential of my developing abilities.

"I have two questions. First, when can I undergo the ceremony to acquire these powers? Second, how long until Crazy Deer launches his next attack?" I inquired, seeking clarity on the timeline.

"I don't know how long it will take for you to gain more power from Mother Earth. She may not deem you ready yet. As for Crazy Deer's next move, I can buy myself some time by pretending to have changed my mind. If I avoid the village and keep my energy low, they may struggle to find me. It's our only chance if you decide to help," Canyon responded, emphasizing the gravity of the situation.

"Let's go in search of Thunder Dog so that I may initiate the ceremony honoring Mother Earth," I proposed, my determination evident in my smile.

Silently, we embarked on our quest to find Thunder Dog, scouring the area in search of him. However, he remained elusive, evading both our physical and energetic senses. After an hour of searching, we concluded that he did not wish to be found. With no signs of his presence, Canyon suggested that I enter his hut to rest.

"I am a little tired, but where will you go?" I inquired, concerned for his well-being.

"I will continue the search for Thunder Dog in the morning. For now, I need to gather my thoughts and find solace," Canyon replied, his weariness evident.

"Rest well, and we will resume our search tomorrow," I said, bidding him farewell as I entered the hut, hoping that the following day would bring us closer to finding the answers and solutions we sought.

"It's better that I stay far away from you and the village. I'll be deep in the forest tonight."

"Good seeing you, dear friend. Everything will be all right," I said with a smile.

We embraced for a long time before I walked into the hut. I watched in the doorway as Canyon disappeared into the forest. A few moments later he had removed all traces of his energy. It was as if he had left the planet - but that was the idea.

While Canyon and I were together, I didn't want to show my concern but now that I was alone there was no need to hide my feelings. I allowed the tears to flow freely. My heart ached for my friend and for our safety. I didn't know if we even had a chance of winning. Many wild thoughts ran through my mind. I walked around talking aloud to myself. "Why am I always the one that has to keep a cool head? How did I get myself into this mess? I'm not a medicine man yet."

I sat on the floor and closed my eyes to meditate. Instantly, my mind, body, soul and consciousness were transformed into many small drops of water positioned high above the clouds in the sky. The drops began to fall softly through the air back toward Mother Earth creating a double spiritual rainbow. The beautiful spectrum of healing colors filled the whole sky.

As the healing sunlight entered my water drops, it refracted and reflected from each drop so that the light created a spectrum of healing colors. The lower the sun descended in the sky, the higher the spiritual rainbow positioned itself above the planet.

My consciousness moved into the rainbow and spread to every color along its bow. In a few minutes the rainbow disappeared and I was sitting back on the floor with my legs crossed.

Then Thunder Dog spoke within my mind. "Tomorrow we will begin the Ceremony Honoring Mother Earth. Don't forget that you're already my apprentice and have many medicine man powers. Don't allow your mind to process any fears. If fear comes up, don't play with it. Let your mind be like water. If you don't stir it, it will become clear and one with the Divine Creator."

Thunder Dog's energy disappeared and our communication was broken. The sun had set behind the mountains and night were fast approaching. I lay on the bed and closed my eyes. Soon sleep came.

Abruptly my body was lifted up off the bed and thrown across the room. With a thud, I landed on the floor near the door. The air felt heavy and had a funky odor. A strong energy was present. I lay motionless as the energy moved slowly throughout the hut. I offered no resistance to the powerful force as it scanned me. It moved closer and hovered over me for a few minutes before disappearing.

The energies of Crazy Dear and Black Horse were at work. They had not found Canyon. I said a prayer that they would not find him, then pulled a blanket from the bed and laid it on the floor. There I lay silently until sleep came to claim me.

Chapter 4

HONORING MOTHER EARTH

Thunder Dog woke me from my slumber with a gentle tug on my shoulder inside Canyon's hut. He urged me to get dressed, informing me that it was nearly 4:00 a.m. and the perfect time to honor Mother Earth. With a sense of urgency in his voice, he emphasized the importance of opening my heart to her, as she may share her special gifts during this ceremony.

Quickly, I dressed myself, realizing that my inquiry about the time was unnecessary. I had already committed to being Thunder Dog and Canyon's guest, participating in their customs and ceremonies. Today, I would undergo a sacred ceremony dedicated to Mother Earth. Breaking free from the habit of constantly checking the time, I stepped outside the hut, greeted by the fresh morning air infused with the scent of honeysuckle. Taking a deep breath, I attempted to fully awaken.

Thunder Dog handed me a canteen of water for the journey, assuring me that Mother Earth would provide more if needed. Grateful, I tied the canteen around my waist and scanned the surroundings for Canyon.

"Canyon won't be joining us today, and I will only occasionally be present in my physical form. You must honor Mother Earth on your own. It is you that she wishes to communicate with. I will accompany you for now, but I will temporarily step away during the journey," Thunder Dog explained.

"I thought I was meant to follow your lead," I responded, puzzled.

"You must discover your own place in this magnificent forest. The special sacred spot that Mother Earth has prepared for you will be revealed solely to you," Thunder Dog assured me with certainty.

"But how will I find that special sacred place without your guidance?" I questioned.

"Simply listen to your inner voice, remain present in each moment, and walk with profound spiritual awareness. Each being on this planet is connected to Mother Earth, dependent on her for our survival. She predates life itself and will remain our mother long after we have transcended," Thunder Dog spoke with deep conviction and reverence.

And so, I began my journey. As I walked for about 30 minutes in the chilly morning air, doubts crept into my mind. You have no idea where you're going, I thought. You're cold, lost, and unhappy. A whirlwind of random thoughts inundated my mind—work, relationships, a Nestle Crunch candy bar, money, sex, and spirituality.

"Buffalo Feather, your thoughts are so loud that they will awaken all the plants and animals in the forest," Thunder Dog chided. "Moreover, happiness resides only in the present moment. The present moment is the only true moment in which you can truly be alive. Today, you must learn to experience the present moment with every step you take. To live your life from a place of spiritual essence, you must learn to walk with awareness of the present moment. Mother Earth will guide you."

"Once you master walking with present-moment awareness and maintain that presence when you return to your everyday world, it will be easier to find your sacred spot anywhere—whether at home, in a bustling city, in an office building, or on an airplane. Wherever you are, your connection to Mother Earth will help you exist in a perpetual state of meditative awareness," Thunder Dog explained.

"I'm trying to stay focused on the present moment, but it's quite cold in the forest at this early hour," I confessed.

"As you walk, allow each breath and each step to be imbued with peace, love, serenity, and inner harmony. Let your walking awaken your very soul. Become one with your breath and your steps... completely and wholly. Allow Mother Earth's love and healing energy to warm you from within," Thunder Dog advised, offering guidance for my journey ahead.

While walking, I directed my focus to my breath and footsteps, and immediately the incessant chatter in my mind subsided. Ahead, I spotted a group of magnificent deodar cedar trees. Their weeping branches and soft green foliage bestowed upon them a remarkable beauty among evergreens. Walking upon their larch-like needles and downy twigs, I felt privileged to be in their presence. Towering over 50 feet tall, these cedars stood as the most elegant among the forest's evergreen inhabitants.

As the sun ascended, its rays warmed the morning air during the hours that followed. I traversed hill after hill, following one trail after another in search of my special spot, but to no avail. Though I maintained present-moment awareness and fostered a connection with Mother Earth, it did not guide me to my sacred place. With each step, I silently offered prayers honoring Mother Earth and poured out my love and deep respect. However, the elusive spot remained undiscovered.

"Can you sense Mother Earth's loving energy enveloping you? Awaken from your dream and experience her vibrant presence," Thunder Dog urged.

A mountain lion stood about 50 yards away on a small hill, observing me closely. Although the mountain lion emanated a powerful spiritual aura, an inner intuition advised me to keep my distance. Surprisingly, I felt no fear, but heeding my inner voice, I continued on my path, allowing the mountain lion to maintain its position on the hill.

Hours passed as I walked further, and the chill of the morning dissipated with the warmth of the midday sun. With the sun shining brightly overhead, I quenched my thirst with a sip of cool water from the canteen. I had been walking for over eight hours, only taking brief pauses. The more I walked, the more I experienced moments of profound unity. At times, I felt fully integrated with Mother Earth and the Divine Creator, only to be interrupted by the intrusion of a passing thought.

A few captivating Sergeant cherry trees stood approximately 20 feet ahead. Reaching heights of over 60 feet, their bark possessed a rich allure. The dark green leaves were transitioning into a vivid red, while the trees bore clusters of deep pink flowers, some adorned with small black fruits. I paused momentarily to appreciate their beauty before resuming my journey.

The sun began its descent, positioning itself lower in the sky. As I walked, I fluctuated between silent, meditative awareness and the intrusion of thoughts that disrupted the stillness. Mother Earth had not yet revealed my special spot, intensifying my determination to honor her and discover it. Throughout the day-long trek, my breaks were brief, consisting only of a quick drink or momentary rest.

To my left, stood several dazzling crepe myrtle trees, their smooth purple bark reaching a height of about 25 feet. To my right, closed pincushion flowers stood on graceful stems, measuring approximately two feet tall. The air carried the sweet scent of spearmint, prompting me to search for its source. Observing the area, I located the spear-shaped flowers of the spearmint plant just a few feet away. Adorned with spikes of lavender and white, the plant emitted a fragrant aura. I uttered aloud, "Beautiful Forest, you are truly alive with love and divine energy."

Traversing the living beauty of the forest, I couldn't help but sense the interconnection between its inhabitants. The forest thrived as a cohesive living system, emanating great power and spiritual energy.

Throughout the day, Thunder Dog trailed behind for most of the journey. Frequently, I would glance back to see his whereabouts, only to find him absent. At other times, he would be right behind me, matching my strides. It seemed as though he came and went as he pleased or as he deemed necessary.

I noticed the presence of lungwort sage, its leaves adorned with white spots, each stretching over a foot in length. Nearby, a cluster of Carolina lupines caught my eye. These wildflowers, with their towering stems and three leaflets, stood over five feet tall, infusing the forest with vibrant energy.

The sun began its descent, painting the western sky with a breathtaking sunset. Unable to resist its beauty, I paused my walk and stood there, fully appreciating the moment as I watched the sun slowly disappear behind the verdant forest.

Father Sky came alive with a symphony of radiant colors, resembling a resplendent rainbow adorned with celestial lights. The sun transformed into a glowing ball of yellow spiritual radiance, gradually descending towards Mother Earth. As the sun dipped below the horizon, its hue shifted to a vibrant golden yellow, suffusing the sky with a gentle, yet potent energy.

The vibrant yellow gave way to a vivid orange, then a bright salmon hue, and finally transformed into a soft peach glow. Mesmerized, I witnessed the last remnants of daylight merge with the arrival of night, existing simultaneously in perfect harmony. It was a moment of divine spiritual power, where day and night coexisted in seamless union, free from conflict.

With my legs growing weary, I slowly sank to the ground, leaning against a towering Sequoia tree. Nightfall descended rapidly, and the sky filled with shimmering stars. Thunder Dog had been absent for quite some time, and I found myself growing hungry. My mind fixated on the image of a KitKat chocolate candy bar, which materialized before my eyes. Its reddish-orange wrapper bore the unmistakable "KitKat" label in bold white letters, and at the bottom, the words "crisp wafers in chocolate" were written in yellow. The taste of rich milk chocolate enveloped my senses, so vivid that I felt as though I could reach out and touch it, although I refrained.

From high above in the starlit sky, the soft melodies of a flute wafted through the air, carrying a divine resonance from heaven itself. The forest fell into a hushed silence, as every living creature, plant, and animal, listened intently to the ethereal music. Its healing essence entered my being, its harmonious tones and gentle pitches caressing my mind and soul. In that moment, I became one with the Divine Creator, fully integrated into the sacred vibrations.

An owl perched in a tree above me, its hoot echoing through the night. I gazed upward, scanning each branch until I spotted the owl about halfway up the tree. It possessed a magical aura, its feathers shimmering under the moonlight. I studied its features, discerning its white breast with reddish-brown bars and a gray tail adorned with five dark stripes, measuring about seven inches long.

As I continued observing the owl, it met my gaze. In that instant, a powerful force lifted me out of my body and into the owl's consciousness. Inside, the owl spoke to me, reassuringly saying, "Do not fear the night, the darkness, or the unseen, for I am the Night Eagle, and I shall bestow upon you some of my potent medicine for your journey. Our union makes it possible for you to receive my powers. I shall return you to your body once the process is complete. With my gifts, you can master the arts of clairvoyance, astral projection, and magic."

Fearless and understanding, I embraced the experience of my consciousness merging with the owl's, embracing its loving and spiritual energy that enveloped me. I recognized this oneness as part of the ceremony preparing me to honor Mother Earth, an essential step on my path to becoming a medicine man. Relaxing into the embrace of the owl's energy, I could feel its power flowing into my consciousness and soul, connecting with my physical body still sitting beneath the sequoia tree in the moonlight.

The owl spoke again, saying, "Look at your physical body, seated there beneath the tree. It is a beautiful vessel, but you can clearly discern that you are not confined to it. With my powers, you can effortlessly transition in and out of your body whenever necessary. While you must honor and care for your physical form, never mistake it for your true essence."

With my consciousness residing within the owl, we took flight, soaring high into the moonlit night. Everything became vividly clear, as night unveiled its secrets with my newfound owl vision. We ascended higher and higher, circling the turtle continent (the Americas) five times. Throughout our journey, we flew over each of the seven continents, and the owl directed my gaze towards a flickering, glowing light below.

Curious, I asked, "What are those flickering lights?"

"They are your brothers and sisters from around the world. They too are participating in the ceremony honoring Mother Earth and receiving their medicine powers. After the ceremony, those who are ready will become medicine men, medicine women, masters, shamans, sorcerers, wizards, swamis, and many other names. The specific titles may vary depending on their geographical location, but the spiritual purpose remains the same. All of you are being awakened to trigger the awakening process in others. While you cannot force enlightenment upon another person, you can use your powers to initiate the enlightenment process if they are open to it. From this moment forward, you will share a deep bond of love with the entire world. You will feel compelled to share your spiritual love with all of humanity."

"I can feel their energy flowing towards me, and my energy connecting with each of them," I responded.

"That is because you are spiritually interconnected. After tonight, you can draw upon their powers, insight, and wisdom indefinitely. Likewise, they can tap into your spiritual energies. You are not alone on this journey; you have abundant support and love as you fulfill your purpose," the owl explained as we continued our flight around the world.

"The day embodies masculine energy, while the night represents the feminine. Did you notice how the night patiently awaited the completion of daylight during the sunset? The night is not aggressive nor in a hurry for daylight to vanish. Instead, the night readily joins forces with the day. You witnessed a beautiful dance and a spiritual union between day and night. Both male and female energies coexist as one within the Divine Creator. Enlightenment can only be attained when you are receptive, in a feminine mood. You cannot conquer the Divine Creator; you can only invite Him in by relinquishing resistance and quieting the mind, allowing spiritual energy to flow within you," the owl elucidated.

The owl's powers permeated my mind completely, elevating my awareness and filling my heart with love. A profound affection for humanity emanated from me, manifesting as tears that fell upon my brothers and sisters below, intensifying and brightening their flickering lights. Observing my fellow beings, I felt our love merge into a harmonious unity. Our souls intertwined as I soared high above Mother Earth in the heavens.

After circling the planet once more, the owl and I returned to the Sequoia tree, where our journey had commenced. As the owl settled on a branch, it spoke, "Now, you possess my medicine powers to guide you on your journey. Use them wisely."

With those final words, my spirit swiftly returned to my physical body, still seated beneath the mighty Sequoia tree. I sat on the warm earth, my eyes closed, surrendering to a deep, dreamless slumber.

The gentle touch of the morning sunlight awakened me, filling me with the vibrant energy of a new day. The air carried the aroma of blueberries, and the taste of blueberries lingered in my mouth. My hands were stained with their juice. Instead of being beneath the Sequoia tree, I found myself beside a bountiful blueberry bush. Rejuvenated and eager to continue my journey, I stood up, greeted by the presence of Thunder Dog standing a few feet away. I was uncertain of when he had returned or how long he had been there.

"Good morning," Thunder Dog greeted me with a refreshed voice.

"Good morning to you. I sense that it is time to resume our search for my sacred spot," I replied, offering a loving smile as I rose to my feet.

And so, I began walking eastward, with Thunder Dog trailing behind me. As I walked, moments of profound oneness would wash over me, allowing me to merge completely with Mother Earth and the Divine Creator. However, occasional thoughts would interrupt the stillness and silence, disrupting the unity.

"I can sense those moments when you are fully connected with the Divine Creator. Do not allow your idle thoughts to sever that connection. Do not resist your thoughts, but instead let them flow freely through your mind, unhindered by the desire to control them. During each of these moments, you face a crucial choice—you can either turn towards the mind or turn towards meditation. Surrender to meditation. Embrace the existential moment. Let go of the past, freeing yourself from moments that have already passed. With each step, feel as if you are born anew. Embrace the joy of simply being," Thunder Dog lovingly guided me.

"I am striving to remain fully present in the moment," I affirmed.

"Buffalo Feather, let your thoughts be like the wind passing through an open and empty hut. An open and empty hut offers no resistance to the wind. Allow your thoughts to come and go, but keep your mind empty," Thunder Dog gently instructed me.

Thunder Dog trailed about 10 feet behind me as I walked in silence, still unsure of where I was headed. My only objective was to find my sacred spot within this vast forest. A wild turkey caught my attention as it strolled a few feet away, its unique feathers captivating my gaze. Curious, I decided to follow it until it disappeared into the thick vegetation.

Glancing around to see if Thunder Dog had noticed the turkey, I discovered his absence. I wondered how long he had been gone, but then I opened my awareness and consciousness, hoping to communicate with him.

"Let your divine love emanate from your core and feel the pulsating aliveness of Mother Earth beneath your feet," Thunder Dog's voice resonated. "Become fully aware of your connection with Mother Earth. You are walking upon her spiritual essence—her flesh, her soul. Experience her divine energy permeating your feet and flowing throughout your entire being. Feel her energy merging with yours and ascending towards Father Sky. Unite with the entire plant and animal kingdom, for they possess potent medicine to share with you on this extraordinary day." His words resonated within me on multiple levels of my existence.

"The crucial aspect is to open your mind, remaining attuned to your walking and embracing the movement of your entire body. Couple your awareness of walking with an awareness of breathing. Remember, you are not walking towards a destination. Discovering your special place in the forest becomes effortless when you have nowhere to go. Bring your focus to your walking and embrace the present moment."

Mother Earth's energy and profound love coursed through every fiber of my being—body, mind, and soul. I felt in perfect harmony with Mother Earth, as well as the plant and animal kingdom. At some point, my physical form dissolved, leaving only the rhythm of breathing, the act of walking, and my spiritual essence. I became completely unified with everything in the forest, and my perception of time seemed to vanish. Each moment unfolded as a fresh creation, untethered by the past or future.

At a certain spot, I sensed the ground moving beneath me. This movement wasn't alarming, like that of an earthquake; rather, it felt akin to a warm embrace or a loving caress. Instinctively, I knelt down on both knees and pressed my lips to Mother Earth's living flesh. In that intimate act, Mother Earth enveloped me with her nurturing energy as I lay face down in the dirt. Suddenly, my garments vanished, and Mother Earth enfolded me within her energetic embrace. I felt warmth, security, love, and above all—I felt at home. This was the spiritual space that Mother Earth had prepared for me.

"Open yourself up to me and allow my healing energy to flow into you," a wonderfully solemn voice resounded.

I recognized it as Mother Earth speaking to me, and my heart brimmed with love, tears streaming down my face. I sensed Mother Earth's profound affection for all of humanity and her sorrow over the harm inflicted upon her body and the environment.

Extending my arms and legs as far as they could reach, I relished the embrace of Mother Earth. Her body exuded tenderness, warmth, and love, while the air surrounding me carried a scent of cleanliness and freshness.

I spoke to her, my voice filled with sincerity, "Mother, I deeply apologize for all that we have done to your body and the environment. It saddens my heart. Though I have taken steps to raise human awareness about the importance of caring for the environment, I realize I could have done more to protect you. In the future, I promise to do better."

"Buffalo Feather, you are more than your physical body, and I am far greater than mere earthly matter. Open yourself to me and merge with me. Experience the potent healing energy that flows within me. I know your heart and soul," Mother's soothing voice echoed within my mind and soul.

As I lay there, I allowed my energy to radiate outward from my body and heart in all directions. Then, I extended my loving energy deep into Mother Earth's core and upwards towards Father Sky. Instantly, I sensed a profound connection forming among the Divine Creator, Mother Earth, Father Sky, and myself.

"I am aware of the power and potential within me to create a healthy environment. I understand that my power and potential are magnified when united with you, Mother. I am honored to have you guide my path," I softly murmured, my lips gently pressed against her sacred body.

"I seek a positive and healthy relationship with you, Mother Earth, and I honor your physical and divine essence. Please allow your divine wisdom to flow through my body, mind, and soul so that I may learn the invaluable lessons you have to teach me. I will utilize your wisdom for the benefit of humanity and the advancement of all," I whispered as my body lay flat against Mother's nurturing flesh. I remained still, completely receptive to Mother's loving energy.

Suddenly, the earth surrounding me transformed into a vibrant red hue. A surge of powerful healing energy emanated from the red earth, entering my genitals. I could feel the warmth as the healing energy began to spin within me, starting at the base of my spine. As the red healing energy whirled within me, I gained a deeper understanding of the physical universe and the realm beyond the physical. I also experienced a profound sense of grounding to the earthly plane. The healing energy cleansed my system as it continued its upward journey towards my head. Gradually, the whirling energy departed from my body through the crown of my head, merging with Father Sky. I remained motionless, enveloped in a state of heightened awareness and connection to Mother.

In an instant, the earth shifted to a brilliant orange. An exquisite beam of orange healing energy entered my sacral plexus, causing warmth to spread throughout my body. The healing energy commenced its spin within me, reaching my spleen. As the energy moved within me, I felt a surge in creativity and sexuality. Obstacles in these realms were cleared away as the energy continued its whirling motion. It then ascended towards my head, exiting my body through the crown and merging with Father Sky.

Before I could catch my breath, the earth transformed into a dazzling yellow hue. A radiant beam of yellow healing energy penetrated my solar plexus, surging through my entire being. As it moved within me, it pulsed and throbbed, amplifying my healing abilities. I felt this yellow energy balancing and restoring my physical body as it journeyed upward towards my head. Once in my head, it spun for a brief moment before departing from my body, merging with Father Sky.

Silence enveloped me as I lay on the warm, soft ground in a spread-eagle position. A grayish-brown mouse and a black flying squirrel scurried past my head. An ant crawled slowly down my face, eventually stopping on my upper lip and delivering a bite. Though the ant's bite caused a slight pang, I sensed its potent medicine energy entering my lip and soul. The ant communicated with me, conveying, "You now possess my powers of patience for your journey. Our energies and powers are eternally intertwined. With this gift, you will embody even greater patience as you carry forth your message and teachings. You shall become a great medicine man." The ant then crawled off my lip and onto the ground, leaving a lingering stinging sensation.

In the ensuing stillness, the earth transformed once more, this time into a different color—green. A beam of green energy entered the center of my chest, awakening my awareness and spiritual consciousness as it spun within me.

"My heart is open to you, Mother, and your loving energy flows freely through my body, mind, and spiritual soul. I have surrendered completely, releasing all my fears. Your soothing energy has permeated my emotional barriers, allowing me to experience the purity of my inner heart and a profound connection with the Divine Creator," I whispered softly, my lips pressed against Mother's body. The green healing energy traversed my body towards my head, where it spun momentarily before flowing upward, merging with Father Sky.

Though utterly exhausted, I found complete relaxation on the warm and comfortable ground. A brownish-red rabbit hopped by, its ears moving in unison while its nose twitched incessantly. A large lizard crawled past my outstretched arms. The earth felt warm, affectionate, and pulsating with vibrant energy. I, too, felt enveloped in a warm green embrace, as if draped in a comforting verdant blanket. I was entirely at ease.

Now, the earth shifted to a radiant blue. The blue healing energy entered my throat, spinning and whirling within me. With my focus centered on my throat, I could feel the beam of blue energy rotating and restoring harmony throughout my body, mind, and soul. As the energy ascended towards my head, it spun briefly before departing from my body, similar to the previous energies.

While lying there on Mother Earth, awash in her healing energy, my soul was fully awakened.

A frog hopped onto my right hand and perched there momentarily before leaping onto my back. It settled in the center of my back, and I could feel its medicine powers and energy flowing into me. Instantly, tears welled up and streamed down my cheeks. Initially, I tried to restrain them, but a voice within me gently urged, "Allow the tears to flow. They are sacred tears, and you must learn to honor them. Let them purify your body, mind, and soul as they return to Mother."

Light rain commenced falling from the sky, descending solely upon my body and not the surrounding ground. The sacred waters from Father Sky cascaded onto me, their touch cleansing and preparing me for profound spiritual growth. The rainwater coursed through my body, mind, and soul, and then flowed back to the earth, where Mother lovingly drank in the sacred waters. When she had finished, my body became warm and dry once more.

The frog hopped from my back onto my left hand, and from there, it gracefully descended to the ground, vanishing without a sound.

Once again, I reclined in silence, observing the earth transform into a radiant indigo hue. This luminous indigo energy entered the center of my forehead, positioned just above my nose and between my eyebrows. It commenced its whirling motion, permeating my entire being. Sensations of heightened spiritual awareness flooded my lower brain and nervous system as universal information coursed through me. Vivid images, vibrant colors, and sacred symbols danced before my eyes, accompanied by melodious sounds. My intuitive powers expanded, and I sensed a profound connection between my spiritual essence and the Divine Creator. It felt as if this indigo healing energy resonated with a fusion of red and blue. Guided by a higher power, I became attuned to the divine order governing my purpose and life.

The indigo energy continued to whirl, eventually departing my body through the crown of my head.

Lying there, invigorated and awakened, I surrendered completely, fully present in the moment.

Unexpectedly, a large black and yellow spider emerged from seemingly nowhere and began its descent down the top of my forehead, traversing across my nose. With the spider resting on my nose, my eyes involuntarily began to close. Though I tried to keep them open and move my hands to remove the spider, my efforts proved futile.

In response, Thunder Dog conveyed, "Remain open in mind, body, and soul to Mother Earth and all her children. Trust and receive the blessings of Mother's special gifts." Thus, I allowed my eyes to close, embracing the unity with the spider.

"I bestow upon you my potent medicine to accompany you on your journey," the spider articulated. "Through my powers of weaving, you shall elude entanglement within the illusion of the physical world. Without my abilities, it is all too easy to become excessively entwined with your physical body, the physical world, and its illusions. To live divinely, you must transcend the confines of the physical dimension and embrace your spiritual soul. Utilize my powers to break free from the intricate physical web woven by your conditioned mind and live your life from a spiritual perspective."

I remained motionless, absorbing the spider's message.

"The conditioned mind perpetually weaves a web of physical illusion, captivating and beguiling. Harness my powers to spin a spiritual web of enlightenment and awareness. This spiritual web will assist you in remaining fully present and awakened," the spider continued.

Slowly, it traversed from my nose to the crown of my head, infusing my body, mind, and soul with its potent healing energy. The sensation was wondrous, profoundly curative, and so intense that my body leapt about six inches off the ground several times. As the spider traversed my body, it spun a resplendent spiritual silk web, imbuing me with its formidable healing energy. Finally, it descended from my feet and returned to the ground.

Remaining still, I continued to lie on the ground in tranquil silence. Once more, the earth transformed, radiating a brilliant violet hue. Healing energy permeated the center of my forehead, between my eyebrows. The violet energy commenced its whirling dance, permeating every fiber of my being. As it coursed through me, it mended my physical body before returning to the crown of my head, where it continued its mesmerizing spin.

The sun positioned itself high in the sky directly above my head and filled the sky with bright white energy. I sensed the power within this great energy and its spiritual intelligence. The white energy seemed to hold a combination of all colors within it. A beam of white healing light extended down to the earth and positioned itself about six inches in front of my head. This wonderful beam of healing energy spun as it flowed from the heavens into the ground.

I lay there unable to move as the healing violet energy continued to whirl within the top of my head.

The beam of healing white light suddenly entered my body, mind and soul through the top of my head. Once inside of my head, the healing white and violet energies joined and whirled together as one within me. The two energies moved throughout my body, mind, and soul, cleansing and healing me as they moved freely. My spiritual powers and awareness increased as the energy whirled throughout me.

A great connection formed between the Divine Creator, myself and all within the universe. I felt total integration with the Divine Creator. My great love for all of humanity increased as the healing energy whirled. My divine connection with Mother Earth and Father Sky strengthened.

A powerful divine light and a deep love flowed throughout my total being. This divine light and loving energy expanded outward to everything around me. I was at one with the Divine Creator and I was fully conscious.

Suddenly, my body left the ground. A powerful source of energy slowly rotated my body until I was standing upright. It elevated me into the air until I was about three feet from the ground. A powerful stream of healing energy flowed from the ground into the bottom of my feet. The powerful healing energy moved upwards through my body, out of the top of my head, and floated to Father Sky in the heavens. The experience was deeply spiritual and my consciousness was dancing with spiritual awareness.

The exchange of healing energy from Mother Earth to Father Sky continued through my body. Ominous black clouds gathered and I wondered what was happening. A huge hand holding a sacred water vase came from out of the cloud and began pouring water on me. As the holy waters fell on me, a voice high in the heavens said, "This ceremony has purified your mind, body, heart and soul. Mother Earth's spiritual powers and many totem animals are available to guide you on your journey. All the animals that you have encountered in this ceremony have given you some of their sacred medicine to support you in fulfilling your spiritual purpose."

The spiritual force slowly lowered me to the ground. Instantly my clothing returned and Thunder Dog said, "Welcome back from your ceremony, Buffalo Feather. Mother Earth, medicine animals and the Divine Creator have all endowed you with their special gifts. You can use their powerful medicine to guide your path and illuminate your journey. Always walk with a meditative silence. You are now truly a powerful medicine man."

We began walking back to the village.

"It took three days and two nights to find your spiritual place in the forest," Thunder Dog said.

"Three days and two nights," I exclaimed. "I only remember two days and one night. What did I do for a day and a night?"

"When the time is right, you will remember that part of the ceremony," Thunder Dog answered with a smile.

"What do I do now? How do I begin?" I asked.

"Just stay conscious and aware. That is enough. There is no doing. It's all about being. Being conscious is your spiritual purpose. It's the way that you will help bring enlightenment into the world." As Thunder Dog spoke, I saw Canyon waving to us from the village.

Chapter 5

POWER OF THE FEATHER

"Thunder Dog, Canyon, and I made our way toward the village," I began.

Canyon, curious, asked, "Did you receive any special powers?"

"He received many wondrous gifts from Mother Earth and Father Sky. But I think it's best for you two to discuss your plans for dealing with Crazy Deer," Thunder Dog interjected. He swiftly vanished into the forest.

"Yes, over the past few days, I have learned many things from Mother Earth," I replied. "These powers can aid us in addressing the situation. Let's talk about it." We found a comfortable spot beneath a fragrant evergreen tree and sat down. The warmth of the sun dancing upon my body felt delightful.

Canyon shared, "I was in the woods, listening to nature and drawing strength from her power. It's time for me to confront Crazy Deer and find a resolution. If I hadn't promised to wait for your return, I would have returned to my hut to prepare for the upcoming energetic battle."

"It's commendable that you're ready to confront your fears, but Crazy Deer and Black Hawk are not the true source," I explained.

"What are you saying?" he asked, his expression turning grim.

"The true fear lies within your mind. It's your resistance to extending love that generates these feelings of fear. Terror has taken hold of you. However, you can never resolve the problem with Crazy Deer from a place of fear. The fear itself is illusory. You have been battling something that doesn't truly exist," I clarified.

Desperate, he pleaded, "What can I do?"

"The first step is to stop regarding your fear of losing Jasmine as a problem. Understand that love is the real answer. Whenever you feel fear of losing Jasmine arising, immediately allow love to flow from your connection to the Divine Creator. Would you allow me to guide you through a process that will open your heart and dispel any fear?" I offered.

"Are you suggesting we do it right now?" he asked.

"Yes, right now. Let me guide you through a process that will release fear and create space for love to flow within you," I affirmed.

"Okay, let's do it. I am ready. I trust you, my brother," he consented.

"Please take a seat on Mother Earth. Close your eyes. Relax your body completely. Allow your thoughts to relax each muscle in your body. Feel the tension dissipating. Focus on your breath. Let love gradually build within you," I instructed.

Canyon closed his eyes, and his positive and loving energy began to expand slowly. A radiant ruby-red aura formed around him.

"I can feel your loving energy emanating from your soul," I whispered softly.

His aura shifted slowly, transitioning into a reddish-orange hue.

"Keep your eyes closed and direct your loving energy toward everything within a fifty-meter radius," I guided.

The air carried the scent of healing balm, and a warm reddish-orange glow enveloped the entire surroundings.

"Your loving energy is growing within you, spreading outward to encompass everything within a one-mile radius. Let powerful love permeate the environment without exceptions. Everything is interconnected within the Divine Creator, and everything is love," I continued.

Once again, his aura changed colors, this time turning into a vibrant yellow.

"Now, extend your love to everything within a two-mile radius, without limitations. Feel your potent energy radiating out to all of humanity," I encouraged.

"I can't consciously push my love any further," Canyon confessed.

"Don't push it. Instead, reconnect with your inner being. Allow your love to build within you. It will naturally overflow and extend itself. You have an infinite reservoir of love to share with the world. The more love you hold within, the more it will naturally radiate outward. Focus on your connection with the Divine Creator, and let your love flow abundantly to all," I reassured him.

His resistance dissolved, and his radiant love began to flow freely, enveloping the entire environment. The air became infused with the scent of fresh ambrosia, and his yellow aura spread across the sky.

It was a marvelous sight to witness his divine transformation. Layer by layer, fear fell away from him, leaving only love. I couldn't help but smile. This was the Canyon I knew – a courageous and peaceful warrior. We sat in a serene silence, basking in the energy that surrounded us.

Gradually, his aura shifted to a soothing yellowish-green hue.

"Now, send your love to Jasmine. Feel it flowing towards her, surrounding her beautiful body. Extend your green light to embrace her," I instructed.

"My loving green light is encompassing her. I can feel Jasmine's presence. We are in communication. I can sense her passionate love. She truly loves me! I had no reason to doubt her love," he exclaimed, filled with surprise.

"Feel her loving energy. Allow any fear surrounding Jasmine to dissipate. Embrace the divine connection between you two," I encouraged.

"She wants you to join our connection and be in communication with us," he added.

I focused my consciousness on their energetic connection and quickly sensed Jasmine's weakened, yet loving energy.

"Buffalo Feather, my native name is Morning Dove," she spoke. "I sent you the dove feathers because, at the time, I couldn't directly communicate with Canyon. It was the only way I knew to send him my love. Those feathers carry all my powerful medicine, which has grown stronger under your care. I didn't want to risk Crazy Deer finding a way to drain my powers. I knew Canyon needed both our powers to defeat him. Now, our period of separation has ended, and we are allowed to be joined."

Instantly, I transported the dove feathers from my car into Canyon's hand. His fingers held them firmly. The air carried the fragrance of fresh cut jasmine, and a gentle breeze caressed my face.

"When two people share the depth of love we do, they must trust in its power," Canyon expressed. "Sometimes situations may seem bleak, but we must have faith in the divine plan. We should not question every detail, but instead believe in the power of love. Our fear will dissolve."

"Canyon, I don't want my powers to be used to harm Crazy Deer," Jasmine interjected. "I am entrusting them to you so that you can convey my choice and my path. I stand for peace, joy, and love, and that must always be the intent behind the use of these powers. I must depart now because my energy is too low to continue. Don't expend any more energy trying to communicate with me. Save your strength to resolve the conflict with Crazy Deer. I love you deeply, and we will be together soon. Buffalo Feather, thank you for your assistance and for being an exceptional spiritual teacher. You will forever hold my love and gratitude. From this day forward, I will be known as Morning Dove, daughter of Naomi, a great medicine woman." With her final words, she severed the connection with us and transferred the remaining power into the feathers. We sat in reflective silence for a long while. Morning Dove's selfless actions stirred profound emotions within me. She had relinquished all her power to be with her divine partner, fully aware that if Canyon failed, she would never regain her power. Her willingness to risk everything in the name of love and peace fortified my determination.

"We cannot fail her," I declared.

"We will succeed," Canyon affirmed.

"Now, close your eyes and focus on the feathers. Feel their love and power. Allow their loving energies to flow freely within you. Let Morning Dove's love merge with your soul. Send your energy outward to everything within a three-mile radius. Fill the entire environment with your energy," I instructed.

The air carried the scent of sorrel, and Canyon's aura transformed into a radiant blue, gradually fading into a softer indigo. Indigo light illuminated the sky, bathing us in its gentle glow.

"Experience your connection with the Divine Creator. Feel the love within you flowing outward to all. Allow this energy to cleanse your entire being completely. Let your healing energy dissolve any remnants of fear," I guided him.

Now the air smelled of sage. Canyon's aura changed to a bright white light engulfing violet beams. The white light quickly filled the whole sky. His medicine powers were growing steadily stronger.

"Let your consciousness search out Crazy Deer. Do not attack him. Instead, send him your love," I said.

After only a few minutes Canyon said "I have found him. I can feel his anger.

"Don't respond to his anger. Keep your love pouring outward," I said. "Allow your mind and your heart to reach out to him. I can feel him and Black Hawk."

"I'm going to bring Crazy Deer here for a talk," Canyon said.

"OK, I will keep Black Hawk from interfering," I said.

Immediately, Crazy Deer was standing in front of us with his mouth wide open. Canyon extended his white aura until it surrounded Crazy Deer.

I focused my energy onto Black Hawk. And before he could take any action, my white light totally surrounded him. He tried to resist, but the more he struggled the stronger my energy field trapped him.

"Don't fight against my powers. I will not harm you. We must allow Crazy Deer and Canyon to find their true pathway. They must discover the truth about the role Morning Dove will play in their lives," I said within his mind.

Black Hawk increased his power hoping to break my energetic hold. Without delay, I transported him and myself back in time to the open plains. It was also the land of thunder that made everything contrary. Here everything worked backwards. In this land you had to roll in the dust to "wash" and immerse yourself in water to "dry off." You said "yes" when you meant "no" and vice versa. To obtain anything, you had to do the opposite of what you wanted.

There were animals and plants all around him. The whole environment operated normally unless Black Hawk tried to do something. A herd of black buffalo was grazing all around him. Each animal had a large eagle feather on its back with my energy flowing through it. Every time he tried to escape, he ran into my energy and the contrary effect. He continued to struggle as I returned to Crazy Deer and Canyon.

Crazy Deer tried to break Canyon's hold on him, but Canyon squeezed the dove feather in each hand which increased his powers. The energy dropped Crazy Deer to his knees.

"We must talk." Canyon said. "You can't defeat me. Clearly you can see that Morning Dove has made her choice. Surely you can feel her power flowing through the feathers. You are strong, but your power is no match for the two of us. I promised her that I would not harm you and I will honor my words. I will release you, so we can resolve this situation peacefully."

"How can we resolve this?" Crazy Deer said. "I saw Morning Dove with me in my vision. I must follow my destiny, even if it means death."

"I don't know what you saw, but I think we should try and find out. Let's pray together and ask the Divine Creator to show us the way. I love Morning Dove more than life itself, but I will give her up if my vision was wrong," Canyon said.

"It's clear that you love Morning Dove, but I do too. I can't see my life without her. I don't know if I have the courage to risk losing her again," Crazy Deer said.

"We must call on the spirit world to help us find the right path. You're a great warrior and someday you will be a great leader. I don't know what the outcome will be, but it's necessary that we risk it." Canyon said.

"You're right, we must discover our path. I have a great vision to achieve. It will be better if I join with you to figure it out," Crazy Deer said.

"We need Buffalo Feather to help us. His energy will allow us to enter the spirit world. Will you allow him to act as medium?" Canyon asked.

"Yes, please help us, Buffalo Feather. We must find our destiny," Crazy Deer said.

"Before I help you get to the bottom of the mystery, I need to release Black Hawk," I said. "We need his powerful magic to support us. Crazy Deer, you must tell him that everything is all right when he returns to this time."

"Okay. Black Hawk will follow my command," Crazy Deer said.

I released the energy surrounding Black Hawk, allowing him to move forward in time. When he joined us, Crazy Deer explained the situation and our agreement, commanding Black Hawk to follow my directions. After a few minutes, Black Hawk nodded in agreement and silently took a seat beside Crazy Deer.

Then, I positioned myself on the ground, halfway between Crazy Deer and Canyon. At my request, Black Hawk manifested a drum, utilizing his remarkable powers of manifestation. The drum appeared instantaneously, and he began beating a slow, spiritual melody, reading my thoughts and responding intuitively. Our minds united, creating a powerful energy field that enveloped us like a comforting blanket.

I instructed Crazy Deer and Canyon to begin singing the spirit calling song, and they obediently joined in, aligning their voices with the rhythmic beat of the drum. As I called upon the Divine Creator for guidance in resolving the problem, my ego gradually dissipated, and my vibration increased. The balance between my femininity and masculinity was restored, eradicating all traces of hatred and antagonism within me. Suffering and pain ceased to exist.

The drumbeat grew stronger and faster, while the tone of Crazy Deer and Canyon's chanting shifted. It was no longer a mere recollection from their memories; instead, they became the embodiment of the song and the dance.

Our thoughts merged in communion, and as our consciousness merged into a single spiritual mind, the Divine Creator manifested as swirling blue-green lights within the energy blanket. Our collective consciousness connected with the Divine Creator, and we sensed the presence of Thunder Dog and Mourning Dove.

"I have joined you to show you the way," the Divine Creator spoke. "Your courageous actions and open hearts reflect your readiness to receive help. The problem arises from perceiving yourselves as separate individuals, detached from one another and me. Deep desires and worldly passions have ensnared you. It is my will that Morning Dove and Canyon unite in marriage through the sacred pipe. They have a great purpose to fulfill in their union, and their souls are already intertwined."

A moment of silence followed as we processed this information.

"Mourning Dove will sit at the head of the Council of Chiefs alongside Crazy Deer. He requires her wisdom to become a great leader of his tribe. It is his destiny to do so. These are challenging times for all people, and strong leadership is crucial. Even the red man finds it challenging to live a spiritual life," the Divine Creator conveyed.

The air carried the fragrance of sage, and a majestic eagle soared across the sky, its wings creating the sound of thunder.

"Black Hawk and Buffalo Feather, you have much to teach each other about being medicine men. Instead of choosing peace and discovering the true purpose of your meeting, you engaged in battle. Your powers must be used for healing, guided by deep wisdom. Having strong medicine alone is insufficient. Spiritual insight and discipline are also essential. Summon the courage to utilize your gifts for the highest good. Remember that the honor of one is the honor of all. You are forever bound as brothers, despite past events. Each of you is responsible for the growth of the other," the Divine Creator emphasized.

The air was filled with the invigorating scent of fresh spearmint, and a mountain lion swiftly crossed our path.

"You have all witnessed the same vision through a unified spiritual mind. There should be no doubt about the path to take. I leave you, as always, with free will to choose any path you desire. Know in your hearts that you are never alone; I am always with you," the Divine Creator concluded. The blue-green light vanished, along with the essences of Mourning Dove and Thunder Dog.

As the medium for the calling, my consciousness was the first to slip away, followed by the others. We sat in silence for a moment, everything becoming clear. The great mystery had been dispelled; it was merely our minds playing tricks.

"I would be honored to have Morning Dove join me at the Council of Chiefs," Crazy Deer expressed. "I need her wisdom and power. She commands the respect and admiration of everyone. Moreover, she will be a wonderful wife for Canyon. I will no longer interfere. Though I will always love her, I will honor your union."

"I agree," Canyon replied. "Mourning Dove will be a wonderful companion for you at the council meeting. She possesses many remarkable gifts that she can share with all of us. Crazy Deer, if you are willing, I would like to invite you to participate in the wedding ceremony. I respect your love for Morning Dove, just as she respects you."

"I'm not sure if I have the strength to attend your wedding. However, please understand that my absence does not signify any disrespect toward your union," Crazy Deer responded, his voice filled with emotion.

We sat in silence for a few moments, allowing the weight of our emotions to settle.

"Now that Thunder Dog has witnessed the union of Mourning Dove and Canyon, let us prepare for the Ceremony of the Pipe," I joyfully suggested.

We made our way swiftly to the village, with Crazy Deer and Canyon walking side by side. Black Hawk and I followed closely behind.

"How did I manage to escape from the place you sent me?" Black Hawk grinned mischievously.

"Now that we are brothers, I suppose it won't hurt to share," I chuckled.

Black Hawk and I exchanged stories about our respective training experiences. While there were many similarities, there were also some differences. I sensed the strength of his power and knew he would become a great medicine man. When we arrived at the village, we sought out Thunder Dog.

"When can we hold the wedding ceremony?" Canyon inquired eagerly.

"You may have the ceremony tomorrow. We are already making preparations. However, you must complete your tasks before we can commence," Thunder Dog informed us.

Crazy Deer and Black Hawk bid their farewells and departed for their village. Canyon and I watched as they disappeared into the dense forest.

"I need to return Morning Dove's powers to her. She is energetically weakened," Canyon stated.

We entered Morning Dove's hut, finding her lying on the bed, looking frail and sickly. Canyon took a seat on one side of the bed, while I sat on the other. He gently placed the feathers on her chest, directly over her heart, and held her left hand while picking up her right. We began to pray.

A surge of potent energy flowed from Canyon into Morning Dove. I could feel her body and spirit coming alive once more. A soft white glow slowly enveloped her, and her aura expanded by about six inches. As her energetic vibration heightened, so did her intelligence, awareness, and vitality.

The feathers gradually merged with her heart and vanished, replaced by a dense energetic substance. It formed a figure-eight pattern over her solar plexus, its tone, color, and rhythm shifting in sync with her increased vibrational frequencies. After about five minutes, it dissipated.

Mourning Dove opened her eyes and smiled at both of us. I could sense her renewed strength within.

"She is back with us," Canyon exclaimed, a smile spreading across his face.

"I have returned from a long journey," Morning Dove spoke. "Now, we can join in peace. I hope my role in Crazy Deer's life brings you happiness."

"I am more than happy. I love you," Canyon expressed warmly.

Mourning Dove stood up and walked around the room, fully recovered and brimming with vitality.

Chapter 6

THE SACRED UNION

"Buffalo Feather, would you be able to stay for the ceremony?" Mourning Dove asked. "I know you've been away from home for a long time, but can you extend your stay a few more days?"

"I will stay," I replied with a smile.

"Buffalo Feather and I need to go prepare for the ceremony. You should also get ready,"

Canyon interjected, kissing Morning Dove affectionately.

Canyon and I walked over to his mother's hut, where she was diligently working on a costume. He explained, "According to our customs, my mother and I are responsible for creating Morning Dove's marriage costume. We have spent weeks spinning cotton and weaving it into two blankets and a white-fringed belt. I have also made a set of white leggings and a pair of white moccasins for her. She will wear this costume only twice, once for our wedding and again for her burial."

As they continued their work, I settled into a comfortable chair. Hours passed until it was early morning.

"We are finally done," Canyon declared.

"It's absolutely beautiful. I will keep it safe until the time of the ceremony," his mother assured him. He nodded appreciatively, and we returned to his hut.

Canyon wrapped his naked body in a warm blanket, and I followed him to Morning Dove's hut. He began serenading her with love songs, playing a flute with grace. After a few minutes, Mourning Dove emerged from the hut, also draped in a blanket. Canyon continued to play the enchanting melodies until she invited him to let go of his blanket and join her in the warmth of hers. They professed their deep love for each other and discussed their future.

The couple gently explored each other's bodies with their hands, their spiritual and sexual energy intertwining as they kissed. Canyon delicately placed the flute on the ground, lifting Morning Dove as she released her blanket. The moonlight bathed their naked bodies, blurring the boundaries between them.

"We are one, and we stand together always," Canyon declared.

"We will forever be united as divine partners on our earthly and spiritual journey,"

Mourning Dove affirmed.

Canyon carried her back into her candle-lit hut, and after a moment, he extinguished the flame. I picked up the blankets and the flute and returned to Canyon's hut.

Eventually, I sensed Canyon speaking to me.

"You have been teaching me the power of observation and the importance of understanding my broader purpose. If you wrap yourself in our blankets, the wisdom of that message will integrate into Morning Dove's and my union," he explained.

I settled into the bed and covered myself with the blankets, feeling their energy coursing through me. Our energies merged and integrated. My body relaxed, and soon I drifted into sleep.

After a few hours, Mourning Dove and Canyon entered the hut, waking me up. "Get up. You must come with us," they urged.

I quickly got dressed and followed them to a clearing in the forest, where Thunder Dog and a woman I had never seen before were waiting.

"This is Naomi," Thunder Dog introduced. "She is a medicine woman and Morning Dove's mother. We require Naomi's powerful medicine to successfully conduct the Ceremony of the Pipe."

Thunder Dog and Naomi washed Morning Dove's and Canyon's hair in a single basin, symbolizing the merging of their lives and spirits. The air carried the scents of sage and wild roses, while a dove flew overhead, cooing.

Mourning Dove and Canyon then made their way to the edge of the mesa to continue solemnizing their union by offering prayers to the sun. Once they finished, they returned to Canyon's mother's hut, where his mother adorned Morning Dove in the marriage costume and braided her hair.

Meanwhile, Canyon and I went to his hut, where we dressed in our own costumes. He wore a vibrant, multicolored marriage shirt adorned with quillwork. The shirt extended down to his knees, with brightly colored beads interwoven with the quills. It appeared to be quite heavy, weighing five or six pounds.

On his feet were red moccasins with an elaborate yellow bead design, resembling small triangles. He looked ceremonial.

He wore the same exotic necklace that he had on the first time we met. A closer look at it revealed a small stone buffalo with a feather carved on its back and a turquoise dove. It was beautiful.

I wore a lazy stitch, long buckskin shirt, with a small double saddlebag. My moccasins were green and white with colorful beads on the soles and uppers. A multi-strand necklace of shells, beads and turquoise chips completed the outfit.

When the wedding was over, Canyon would save and protect both of our costumes. Upon his death they would be burned along with his body and other personal belongings in a ceremony honoring the dead.

We walked to the sacred joining circle at the edge of the main camp. Thunder Dog and Naomi were standing at the head of the circle.

Before long the council of the elders and members of the whole village were standing in the sacred circle. Each person placed a gift or said a prayer in a special area at the right front of the circle. Mourning Dove and Canyon's mother were the last to join the circle. Mourning Dove took her place next to Canyon and I stood slightly behind them. We faced Thunder Dog and Naomi.

My emotions ran high and I was filled with love. There was excitement in the air, as most of the people in the circle had never experienced a Ceremony of the Pipe. Each person knew what a special gift it was to participate in this type of divine joining.

The ceremony began with Thunder Dog loading tobacco into the pipe. The pipe had a delicately crafted six-foot-long stem, decorated with fur, horsehair wrappings, and quills. It also had a small hawk, dove and buffalo carved on it. I felt particularly strong powers emanating from it.

Thunder Dog began the ceremony by acknowledging the four directions, beginning with the east.

Thunder Dog stood facing east and held the pipe with its stem pointed eastward in one hand and a pinch of tobacco in the other. Everyone turned and faced east. He sprinkled some tobacco on the ground before putting the rest it into the pipe's bowl. By sprinkling a portion upon the ground, he recognized that we must always give back to Mother Earth part of what we have taken.

"The sun rises in the east, signaling the beginning of a new day for each of us. The east is the direction of renewal and reawakening. It's the place where we learn to believe in what we cannot yet see. Red is the east. It brings us the rising of the sun that brings us a new day and new experiences."

"Lessons from the east will test Morning Dove and Canyon," Naomi said. "These lessons will teach them purity, trust, and hope. Just as the east is the place where light comes into the world, it will also provide them with great guidance and clarity."

Thunder Dog turned to the south and pointed the pipe stem in that direction. He held a new pinch of tobacco slightly above his eye level in a southerly direction. "The south is yellow, a place to receive strength and wellbeing. It is also a place where Mother Earth gives us our growth and development. It is a place of heart, generosity and noble passion."

"The south is the place for preparing," Naomi said. "With the energy from the south, Mourning Dove and Canyon will prepare for their future and provide for the wonderful days ahead. The south will also give them the powers of sensitivity, loyalty and love."

Thunder Dog placed a pinch of tobacco into the pipe bowl. Then he faced west. "Black is the color of the west. It's the place where the sun goes down and darkness comes. Black is the direction of prayer, meditation, deep personal reflection, darkness, release, and spiritual protection."

"The west is the place where Morning Dove and Canyon will receive the powers of perseverance, healing and protection," Naomi said.

Then he sprinkled tobacco upon Mother Earth and put some into the pipe bowl. Every time Thunder Dog faced a direction, everyone in the circle faced that direction as well and listened to his words intently. I also noticed that there were seven people with pipes positioned evenly around the circle. They matched Thunder Dog's actions, movements and words exactly.

He sprinkled tobacco to the north and then inserted it into the bowl. "The last of the four directions is north. White is for the north. It's the place for drawing new wisdom, strength, endurance, purity and truth. Mourning Dove and Canyon will learn the great lesson of the north. You must use the great mountain as a teacher. The way becomes steeper and more difficult as you climb higher on its slopes. Simultaneously, you will see more and become stronger as you ascend. On your journey, the energy from the north will provide you with wisdom, fulfillment, freedom from fear and insight."

"The mystery of all endings is found in the birth of beginnings," Thunder Dog said.

"There is no ending to the journey of the four directions. The human capacity to develop never stops. The medicine wheel turns forevermore. We honor the powers of the four directions always. The gifts of each direction balance other gifts. The boldness of the eagle balances the humility of the willow and the careful wisdom of the turtle. Canyon's idealism and passionate involvement in the world is balanced by Morning Dove's wisdom and clarity of thought."

"Dearly beloved Mother Earth, you are mother to us all. You feed, clothe and house each of us. Every particle of our body comes from you. We honor, protect and love you. Father Sky, your sun energy, brings forth life from Mother Earth. Your union is responsible for all life. We will work hard to return health to both of you by protecting the environment."

Then Thunder Dog made a final offering to the Great Spirit. He held the pipe firmly in the palm of his hand with the stem pointed outward. Then he pointed the stem straight upward, towards the center of the universe. "Our true home is in the center of the universe. It's to the center that we must always return."

Thunder Dog and Naomi turned and faced Morning Dove and Canyon. Simultaneously Crazy Deer and Black Hawk walked out of the forest. They stopped at the edge of the joining circle. Crazy Deer had a tomahawk and arrow in his hand. Black Hawk was carrying some kind of medicine pouch. Thunder Dog looked up at them as everyone turned to see what was going on.

"May we enter your joining circle? Our desire is to honor the sacred union. The gifts are our offerings of respect," Crazy Deer said.

"Come into the circle and join our family," Canyon said.

Thunder Dog motioned with his hand for them to come ahead. They walked to the front of the circle and placed their gifts next to the other presents.

"The gifts are beautiful and we shall treasure them always," Morning Dove said.

Thunder Dog returned his focus to Mourning Dove and Canyon. "It's time to speak the joining words."

"It's the spirit behind the words that binds two souls forever," Naomi said.

"Canyon, I have chosen you as my heart center," Morning Dove said. "Your love will always beat within my heart. We join our minds, bodies and spirits forever as one in this life and beyond."

"Mourning Dove, I have chosen you as my heart center," Canyon said. "Your love will always beat within my heart. We join our minds, bodies and spirits forever as one in this life and beyond."

"You join as one," Thunder Dog said.

"Your souls will always be together. Your spirits join as one," Naomi said.

"Are you ready to integrate your sacred totem animals into your union? After that point there is no undoing of the union," Thunder Dog said.

"Yes, we are ready," they answered simultaneously.

Thunder Dog clapped his hands together seven times, then motioned for everyone to sit on Mother Earth, which we all did.

Thunder Dog stuffed a pinch of some plant, into the pipe bowl. It was not tobacco. He lit it and took a long draw. Naomi accepted the pipe for her draw, then she passed it to Canyon. After his draw, he gave it to Mourning Dove, who handed it to me. Its beauty and power were almost overwhelming. I felt each of their energies and love within the pipe's body. Many of my own loving emotions quickly flowed into the stem. After taking a long, slow draw I felt light-headed and a little woozy. My vision blurred and the people around me became indistinct. If I had not been sitting, I would have fallen. I handed the pipe to someone, possibly an elder.

Out of the corner of my eye, I noticed the seven other pipe holders taking draws from the pipe and passing it around. Each person said a prayer as the pipe made its way from one individual to another. If it was not appropriate for some to smoke, they still said their prayers and the pipe passed over their heads to the next person. The rhythmic beating of the drum resonated with the heartbeat of Mother Earth.

"Oh, Great Spirits, please bless this union by revealing the totem animals that you wish to integrate into the joining of Mourning Dove and Canyon," Naomi spoke, her voice carrying a sacred reverence.

In a mesmerizing transformation, Thunder Dog's body morphed into that of a raven. His form was now dark black, and he moved with the grace and flight of a raven. The air around us carried the scent of blackberries.

"The raven bestows its medicine of magic and the gift of consciousness upon this union. Its powers will aid you in exploring your inner fears and grant you the courage to navigate the darkness of the formless world," Naomi explained.

Next, Naomi transformed herself into a hummingbird, seemingly suspended midair.

"You possess the powers of the great hummingbird," Thunder Dog continued. "This forever connects you to the black sun and the fifth world. Along your journey, you will encounter numerous contradictions and dualities that may drain your energy. This medicine grants you the ability to solve the riddles of duality and hear the celestial music that awakens the joy of living."

Thunder Dog's shape shifted once more, assuming the majestic form of a mountain lion. I marveled at the power exuding from his shoulders as he moved gracefully on all fours.

"The mountain lion imparts the power of leadership," Naomi said. "With this gift, you can harmonize power, intention, strength, and grace. It brings equilibrium to body, mind, and spirit."

Naomi then transformed into the shape of a dragonfly, embodying its essence.

"The dragonfly empowers you to master dream time and unravel the illusions we accept as physical reality," Thunder Dog proclaimed. "It also bestows upon you the ability to undergo transformation, access great wisdom and enlightenment, and call upon the Divine Spirit."

Thunder Dog assumed the shape of a fox.

"The fox carries the message of adaptability in the face of change," Naomi explained. "You can silently observe, remaining undetected and without arousing self-consciousness in others."

Naomi gracefully crouched near the ground, and we all watched in awe as her body morphed from a cocoon to a chrysalis and finally into a butterfly. Thunder Dog provided a narrative as the metamorphosis unfolded.

"The butterfly endows you with the power of transformation, the ability to understand your mind and observe your place in the cycle of self-transformation. It brings clarity to your mental processes," Thunder Dog shared.

With arms outstretched, Thunder Dog flapped them as if in flight, and with each movement, he transformed into a hawk.

"The hawk serves as the messenger of the gods," Naomi affirmed. "With its energy, you will possess keen observation skills, perceiving the obvious in everything. See the big picture in your union and examine it from a higher perspective."

"Mourning Dove, Canyon, please rise," Thunder Dog beckoned.

Canyon spoke from his heart, expressing his lifelong doubts and uncertainties about his identity and belonging. But with Mourning Dove by his side, he felt like an arrow released from a bow, with unwavering clarity and purpose.

"My beloved husband, I will always be with you," Mourning Dove declared, her smile radiating love and devotion.

Mourning Dove and Canyon embraced and kissed passionately, their affection echoing throughout the village. The collective cheer of the onlookers resounded, only ceasing when the couple completed their kiss. Thunder Dog and Naomi presented the ceremonial pipe to Morning Dove and Canyon.

"You now possess the power of the pipe, to draw upon during challenging times or to reaffirm your commitment," Thunder Dog conveyed. "Use it to honor your union. Every full moon, you must smoke the pipe and invoke its powers. If you are apart during that time, the one in possession of the pipe must conduct the smoke and summon the other's spirit."

"Today, you have received many magnificent gifts from Mother Earth and Father Sky in the form of totem magic," Naomi expressed. "It is essential that you integrate these special powers into your marriage, for they are a profound blessing. Let their insights and wisdom guide how you treat one another as you navigate the world."

"Your union is complete," Thunder Dog declared. "It is a closed circle; with the love you share residing in the center of your hearts for all eternity." He clapped his hands together seven times, signifying the completion of the ceremony.

"Let the feast commence!" Naomi announced with enthusiasm.

Everyone returned to their huts, singing and dancing joyously. Food and drinks were brought out, and flute music filled the air as the drummer played a gentle beat.

Mourning Dove and Canyon warmly embraced me and expressed their gratitude to the council of elders, Thunder Dog, Naomi, Canyon's father, Crazy Deer, and Black Hawk. They visited each hut, paying their respects and sampling the various foods.

My attention turned to Thunder Dog, whose face revealed signs of aging and pain. It was the first time I had truly acknowledged his age. Without hesitation, I rushed over and placed his arm around my shoulder. Naomi joined me, and together we slowly walked him to his hut.

"Go and join the celebration," Thunder Dog insisted.

"I can't leave you in this state!" I protested.

"I will stay with him until you return," Naomi assured me. "Everyone is expecting your presence. They wish to honor you and have your blessings grace their homes. The people view you as Canyon's closest friend and divine guide, as well as a revered medicine man. We face many challenges ahead, and your presence serves as inspiration to many. So go, he will be alright for now."

With a heavy heart, I looked at them both. Deep down, I knew that Thunder Dog's illness was serious. Reluctantly, I left their side and rejoined the festivities.

A few young people eagerly took hold of my hand and guided me from hut to hut. At each table, I sampled a small portion of food. Everyone was delighted to have me there, and as I listened to their stories, I realized the profound impact I had made in their lives. It was humbling to hear the tales, for while they spoke of me, I struggled to fully recognize the person they described. It was me, yet also not entirely me. The stories held truth, perhaps embellished, but fundamentally accurate. How had I performed so many acts that had touched and helped countless individuals without fully realizing it? In my heart and mind, I felt compelled to thank them for their special gifts. I honored them and felt blessed to be in their presence, rather than the other way around.

However, Naomi's voice resonated within my mind, guiding me towards a different perspective. "You must accept the fact that the entire village holds immense respect for you as a powerful medicine man. You continue to believe that you have not made a significant impact on their lives, but you do not require grand feats to demonstrate your influence. Your very essence, the way you exist, affects those around you and even those who hear about you. Your divine essence carries great power and spiritual allure. Your words and actions give birth to remarkable stories that people feel honored to share with others. Remember that what may seem insignificant to you in the moment holds great significance to those who observe the accumulation of your words, deeds, and presence. Learn to accept the honor bestowed upon you by others in their own way and embrace your purpose. In time you will discover that your impact is more about your being and not about what you do or have."

I contemplated her words, I found it easier to listen to stories about myself without judgment. I allowed everyone to be as they were without attempting to change them.

The night grew late as I concluded my visits to each family. Emotions surged within me, and the overwhelming love throughout the camp moved me to tears.

The singing, dancing, and feasting continued well into the night, accompanied by the steady beat of the drum. Different drummers took turns, but the gentle rhythm persisted throughout. It was a magical night for all.

At midnight, Mourning Dove and Canyon retreated to their hut to smoke the sacred medicine pipe. A few young individuals played soft, tender melodies on the flute outside their hut, taking turns throughout the night as they had agreed.

As I made my way back to Thunder Dog's hut, my heart brimmed with various emotions. The scent of sage and fresh pine permeated the air, creating a soothing atmosphere.

"How is he?" I inquired upon my arrival.

"He's sleeping," Naomi replied.

Chapter 7

A DEEPER SLEEP

"Let's go outside," Naomi suggested. We walked beneath the night sky, adorned with countless shimmering stars. After a few minutes, we found a spot to rest and admire the beauty of the night. I settled against a sturdy pine tree, while Naomi reclined on her back, gazing up at the celestial display. The scent of sage and fresh wildflowers enveloped us, adding to the serene ambiance.

Curiosity sparked within me, and I asked, "How old is Thunder Dog?"

"He is well over a hundred and eight," she replied.

"A hundred and eight!" I exclaimed in astonishment.

"He has witnessed many harsh winters and countless seasons. I was just a young girl when we first crossed paths, and even then, he was advanced in age. As you observed tonight, he always exudes vitality during ceremonies."

"I never realized his age until today."

"He presented himself to you in the way he wanted you to perceive him. He didn't want his physical appearance to distract you from the task at hand. The Ceremony of the Pipe demanded his complete focus and energy. Assuming the physical forms, movements, and energies of the totem animals integrated into Morning Dove and Canyon's union was a tremendous challenge. Although I am much younger than he is, it still exhausts my body."

"So, for the past two years, he projected a physical form that would ease my training?" I questioned.

"Yes. He sensed your concerns regarding age, and projecting a different physical form is no easy feat. As you witnessed, our bodies and essences transformed into the totem animals. Each of us possesses the ability to project various physical forms and attitudes. We expend significant energy to extend the personality type with which we feel comfortable. Projecting our false selves requires as much energy as projecting a physical form. We often project our illusory personalities without considering the energy it consumes.

"When Thunder Dog identifies a student with great potential, he devotes himself entirely to ensure that person has every opportunity to walk the path of a medicine man or woman. He recognized that his physical appearance could hinder your development, but now he believes you have transcended that issue through your training. And now, he is nearing the end of his life. It is time for his spirit to return home."

"I was unaware of my issues with age or physical appearance. It is fortunate that they have surfaced for resolution, indicating progress on my part. I am grateful for Thunder Dog's guidance during this time. How much time does he have left?" I inquired.

"Just a few more days," she replied softly. "You and I are the only ones aware of his impending passing. I am here to assist him in crossing over to the spirit world. His departure saddens me as well. However,

I am deeply honored to take his place as the tribe's medicine woman. He has entrusted us with a significant request."

"What request did he make?" I asked, intrigued.

"It is a weighty responsibility. He asked me to ensure that your training is completed."

"Please don't take this the wrong way, but why you? Why not the same medicine man who is training Black Hawk?" I inquired further.

"Thunder Dog believes you need to cultivate and align your feminine energy. Due to your strong affinity for the yellow world, he felt that my training in the eastern traditions would be beneficial. I spent five years studying with a revered master in Puma, India. In that part of the world, I am still regarded as a healer and an enlightened one."

"Why did you choose to study in the east when there is so much beauty and spirituality in the west?" I pondered.

"Many years ago, Thunder Dog had a vision that revealed his role in fostering harmony among the different worlds. The Divine Creator instructed him to seek out individuals who possess a divine purpose in integrating the four worlds. I am one of those individuals. Part of my training involved learning and teaching about the unification of the yellow and red worlds. It has become my life's work to demonstrate that nations need not exist in conflict with one another. Realizing this harmonious reality has been my driving force.

"When I initially decided to accept the assignment in India, some questioned my motives. They speculated that I was going there because of the archaeological theory suggesting that Native Americans were originally Asians who migrated across the Bering land bridge over 12,000 years ago."

"How did you deal with that?"

"I told each of them that I was not interested in the works of archaeologists. We as Native Americans have our own story of our origin. It is a journey of spirit, not a tale of the migration of people. Our life begins with the Divine Spirit and Mother Earth, just like the corn planted in the earth that has sustained us for centuries."

"In the east, they welcomed me with open arms. Divine Energy and oneness filled the yellow world. I quickly completed my training, but I stayed longer to teach and continue learning. Thunder Dog's vision proved to be true. We can live in harmony with each other if we develop our spirituality. We are all spirit and earth."

"What did he ask of me?"

"You must tell the elders and others of the tribe that he is dying. He has selected you because you are a powerful example of the different worlds living in harmony. He wants to ensure that everyone knows you were his last student. This will make you even more of a medicine man in their eyes. And, yes, it will add to the stories already being told about you. I know you don't like that. However, whether you like it or not, stories about you will always fill your path."

"I'm learning to stop resisting and let the stories be. However, I can't imagine my life without

Thunder Dog's wisdom and spiritual energy."

"Don't misunderstand me. His energy will be with you always. You can call upon his spirit whenever you want. The time has come for him to leave his body and the physical world. He will reside in the spirit world with the great medicine men and women who have gone ahead. He has supported the people and many great chiefs on his long journey. It's time for him to rest."

Tears streamed down my face as deep sadness invaded my heart and mind. Anguished words poured from my mouth. "I don't want him to go. Surely, it's not his time. We just met. It's only been two years. My training is not complete. His guidance made my path seem so clear. He has taught me so much and now my pain is too great for me to think straight . . . I need some time in silence."

"Thunder Dog told me that you handle things better if you are left alone in silence. So, I will leave you."

"Are you sure doctors can't help?"

"You must understand -- he is not sick. He has no disease. If he were ill, he would heal himself. The time has come for him to release his body. You believe people only die from accidents or sickness, but those are not the only ways to leave this world. Thunder Dog is a powerful medicine man who decided at age forty-three to end all sickness of the body. He has not been ill since. Search your heart and inner knowledge to gain greater awareness of the situation."

"Do you mean he's not in pain?"

"He's not experiencing any physical pain. Many strong emotions fill his heart because he will miss his friends. Also, he knows that everyone will miss him. This causes him deep sorrow."

"I will really miss him . . . a lot," I said, choking up.

"He knows you will. When you left the hut earlier, he felt your deep pain, sorrow and sadness. He is familiar with your emotional state. Your projected stoic personality does not fool him. It's all right to miss him, but understand that he will remain within you always."

"I know he will, but . . ." My tears flowed like a river.

"Don't allow your feeling of sorrow to trap your mind. Remember that nothing is ever born and nothing ever dies. We move between the visible and invisible worlds. When we are invisible, we are in a special resting place. After each day you need a deep sleep to rejuvenate yourself and make you fresh again. In the same way, your body needs death. Think of death as a deeper sleep and nothing else. Thunder Dog's body has been working without a rest for over 108 years. It's not sick, but it is tired. We must simply allow him to return to the divine source."

"He wants us to use the energy created from his death as a great moment of meditation and prayer. Remember, Thunder Dog's life will pass in phases. For a great medicine man, dying takes more time than usual. When his breathing stops, he has only reached the first stage. If his energy level is high at this point, it may take days, or months before all of the life force has passed. This is why I will not cremate his body for at least three months. It's my responsibility to make sure that all his energy has passed before his body is reduced to ashes."

Now, both of us were crying. I rose to my feet and ventured deeper into the woods, seeking solace in the silence that enveloped the forest. My heart weighed heavily, and the tranquil ambiance of the surroundings seemed to understand my need for peace. After a few hours of introspection, I made my way back to the village.

As I arrived, the sun was beginning to rise, and the village gradually stirred with life. I first visited the chief's hut and then proceeded to inform the elders about Thunder Dog's impending passing. None of them appeared surprised, but they all expressed profound sorrow. I went from hut to hut, sharing the news with each family. By the time I reached the last one, they were already aware. No one questioned the reality of his departure. Finally, I returned to Thunder Dog's hut.

"It's good that you have informed everyone," Thunder Dog acknowledged.

"Yes, everyone knows, but..." I hesitated.

"What is it, Buffalo Feather?" Thunder Dog inquired.

"Everyone seemed to accept your passing without question," I explained.

"Oh yes, questioning is futile. Questioning can be a way to avoid confronting death directly. It may provide a false sense of security, shielding one from the inevitability of dying. Native people understand that each of us will face death in due time. It is the destination we all arrive at punctually. Life is truly a journey toward death. Each day, we live and die a little. It is all part of the spiritual plan, a phase of the cycle. Everyone in the village knows that I have lived a long life, and the Divine Creator has bestowed countless blessings upon me. There is no need to question what is. Questioning merely creates illusions. The reality is that it is my time to transition to the spirit world," Thunder Dog explained with wisdom.

The distant sound of the drumbeat seeped into the hut, distinct from the rhythm of the previous night. It now beat for Thunder Dog.

"Do not be alarmed. It is a way of honoring me and signaling to everyone and everything that I am returning to the spirit world. I must venture into the forest to bid farewell to Mother Earth and her realm. Please accompany me," Thunder Dog invited.

He hastily adorned himself in ceremonial attire, and Naomi joined us as we embarked on a walk through the forest. Surprisingly, no one in the village paid any heed to our departure.

"The people understand that today is not about them. They must grant me the time to bid farewell to Mother Earth and the environment that has nurtured me all these years," Thunder Dog explained.

The trees seemed to sway in acknowledgement, and the grassy brush appeared to caress his legs as he passed. Such reactions were absent when Naomi or I walked by.

"Buffalo Feather, all of life is honoring Thunder Dog," Naomi remarked. "He has been a cherished friend and medicine man to all, not solely to humans."

Finally, we reached a beautiful grassy clearing. Towering trees stood majestically in the distance to our left, and a serene lake shimmered just a few yards ahead. On our right, three enormous rocks were positioned about ten feet apart. Each of us settled on the flattened top of a stone. Thunder Dog closed his eyes and commenced singing a prayer song unfamiliar to me.

The ground beneath us trembled gently, and the air carried an unusual, sweet scent unrelated to flowers. Strangely, a light shower descended from the sunny sky. A beam of radiant sunlight bathed Thunder Dog's body.

A mountain lion emerged from behind a tree, approaching Thunder Dog and brushing its furry body against his leg. The creature emitted a resounding roar before sorrowfully walking away. One after another, animals emerged from the forest, passing within a hair's breadth of Thunder Dog before vanishing into thin air. The sky transformed into a swirling aviary as birds of every shape and size circled above Thunder Dog's head, bidding their farewells. His profound connection with all forms of life—plants, minerals, and animals—was unmistakable.

Thunder Dog rose to his feet and gazed at the lake. "Naomi, Buffalo Feather, stay here. I will be back. Whatever transpires, do not follow me. I shall return."

With those words, he began walking toward the lake, pausing at its banks to resume singing.

Curiosity overwhelmed me, and I turned to Naomi. "What is he doing?" I inquired.

"He is bidding farewell to the lake and all its marine life," Naomi replied.

"Marine life?" I questioned, puzzled.

"He is a friend to all bodies of water, whether they are called lakes, rivers, oceans, seas, or by any other name. He is sending his love and farewells to all life forms that reside in or around water," Naomi explained.

"He truly possesses a deep love and reverence for everything. There is so much wisdom to learn from him," I remarked.

"You already know what he knows about loving and honoring everything and everyone. The lessons he has imparted to you over the past two years are but a fraction of his most powerful teaching—to transcend knowledge and embody and live the wisdom he has shared. His greatest lesson is that he lives each day in unity with all in the universe," Naomi enlightened me.

"The logic is there. However, putting it into practice is easier said than done," I admitted.

As Thunder Dog's singing grew louder, a faint scent of wet seaweed wafted through the air. Naomi and I fixed our gaze on Thunder Dog. A fine mist began to form and rise above the lake. It gradually thickened until it enveloped the entire lake and its surroundings. The mist became so dense that Thunder Dog was no longer visible, but his singing resonated powerfully.

We stood there, attempting to catch a glimpse of what Thunder Dog was doing. The mist grew into an impenetrable ten-foot wall, concealing him from our sight. A dolphin, a whale, and a swan gracefully swam upon the mist before vanishing within seconds.

"Did you see that?" I asked, astounded.

"Yes, I saw them. They are aspects of Thunder Dog's totems," Naomi confirmed.

We continued observing the lake for about an hour, but no other manifestations occurred. However, peculiar splashing sounds emanated from the water.

Thunder Dog's singing eventually ceased, and the mist slowly receded back into the lake. He walked back to us and settled on the rock. We sat in silence deep into the night, awaiting the arrival of nocturnal creatures paying their respects. An owl and a bat flew over Thunder Dog's head, leading a procession of other nighttime animals. This procession continued for hours.

"Lie back and allow Mother's love to flow into you," Thunder Dog suggested.

The night air enveloping us felt warm, and a healing heat emanated from the rocks, permeating my body. The enchanted seat conformed perfectly to my body's needs. I didn't feel tired or numb. While the rest of the forest seemed cold, Mother Earth ensured our comfort.

When the sun rose, I awakened, realizing that I had experienced a peaceful, dreamless sleep.

"Good morning, Naomi, Buffalo Feather," Thunder Dog greeted us. "Last night was profoundly special for me. Mother and I had a wonderful visit. I apologize for lulling you to sleep, but I desired to be alone with her. You both must remember all that you witnessed. Now, it is your time to live in accordance with the Divine Creator's guidance and be in harmony with all in the universe."

"I will," we replied simultaneously.

"Naomi, please return to the village and prepare for today's ceremony. I would like to speak with Buffalo Feather," Thunder Dog instructed.

"Yes, I have much work to attend to," Naomi acknowledged, before hurrying away.

"Buffalo Feather, this will be our last conversation in physical form. There are a few things we should reflect upon. I know you already grasp their essence, but it is beneficial to preserve these thoughts in your memory," Thunder Dog began.

"Yes?" I responded, eager to listen.

"Your connection to the Divine Creator is attained through a state of no-thought. Only from this state can you attain the spiritual awareness required to become a great medicine man. In this state, your thoughts will not impede your spiritual growth," Thunder Dog explained.

"Are thoughts considered detrimental?" I inquired.

"Thoughts have their usefulness as they allow you to navigate the physical world. However, you must learn to differentiate between your thoughts and divine guidance. Otherwise, you may mistake everything that arises in your mind as either mere mental chatter or divine wisdom when, in reality, it is often a blend of both," Thunder Dog advised.

"My thoughts often appear so real that it is challenging to discern the difference. It becomes easier as I engage in meditation and prayer, and I am making progress," I shared.

"The practice of consistent meditation dissipates negative energy," Thunder Dog explained. "As this negativism dissipates, your mind is liberated to reconnect with its higher self. From this higher self, you can establish a connection with the Divine Creator, which will support you in mastering yourself. Remember, you can only master yourself and not others. You are accountable for your own actions, thoughts, and life. Although you may seem to have mastery over others, in truth, you can only master yourself."

"I understand that my greatest service to the world is achieved by mastering my own thoughts and living my life in harmony with all," I acknowledged.

"When you are in touch with the peaceful and healing aspects within you, your love will radiate to all. Your five senses will become finely attuned and aligned with the presence of the Divine Creator. Your senses serve as windows to the physical world. Therefore, you must not allow the cold wind to blow through them and disrupt your perception of the goodness within you," Thunder Dog advised.

"I recognize that my perceptions do not necessarily reflect reality. I am learning to evaluate what I perceive with spiritual awareness," I replied.

"Fundamental human nature would lead you to believe that your perceptions are the ultimate reality. If you experience anger, you become the anger. If you experience love, you become love. However, you must not close all your windows, for there are countless miracles in the world. Open your windows to these miracles and observe each one with understanding," Thunder Dog emphasized.

"As I live by the teachings of the Divine Creator, my sensitivity deepens," I stated.

"Remain aware as you sit beside a clear flowing stream, listening to its beautiful music. Yet, do not lose yourself entirely in the stream or the music. It is possible to maintain self-awareness, be conscious of your breath, and still avoid most dangers," Thunder Dog advised.

"I am striving to live according to the teachings of the Divine Creator," I affirmed.

"Buffalo Feather, the initial step toward living by the teachings of the Divine Creator commenced when you sensed that your life held a greater purpose than what you were living out. Your willingness to venture beyond your ordinary world is evidence of this. You asked yourself, 'What is the purpose of life?' Your quest for answers firmly set you on the path of living a spiritual life," Thunder Dog explained.

"You have reached a point in your journey where merely seeking to understand the meaning is no longer sufficient. Deep within your heart, you know that you must transcend reading, studying, and discussing spirituality. You must apply the spiritual laws that you know exist. Your purpose is to love from a profound state of awareness in every moment of your life," Thunder Dog conveyed.

"The time has come for me to live in the present moment, completely connected with the Divine Creator. Before I met you, I knew I desired a teacher. I searched and found you when I was ready to accept your teachings," I expressed.

"Your sincerity and willingness to work with me were the decisive factors in my acceptance of you. I sensed that you had made the decision to seek a teacher, even though you didn't fully comprehend the reasons at the time," Thunder Dog responded.

"I must confess—back then, I didn't fully grasp why I needed a teacher," I admitted.

"Instruction was necessary because you could only perceive your life experiences, attitudes, and opinions through your own perspective. I am guiding you through the hardened mass of what you consider your identity. I am also the embodiment of what I teach. My true purpose is to support you in living from a spiritual perspective," Thunder Dog clarified.

"Thunder Dog, you have taught me the importance of living in alignment with what I speak and what I know. I can no longer live in contradiction with myself. I am living with greater honesty and harmony within myself, without manipulating people or circumstances. This alone brings an abundance of loving energy into all aspects of my life and relationships. The clarity of my intentions has caused all negative conditioning to dissipate and is transforming my life," I shared.

"Excellent, Buffalo Feather. You have made significant progress. You must practice bringing your complete attention to every action you undertake. Being fully present in each moment allows you to be receptive to the Divine Creator's guidance, which is necessary for perceiving reality clearly. Practicing discernment in decision-making prevents you from setting negative events in motion. It is easier to follow the guidance of your higher self than to rectify a mistake," Thunder Dog advised.

"My old belief system no longer holds validity. I have cultivated an awareness of the higher self that is not ego-based. Moreover, I am living in harmony with Mother Earth, Father Sky, and all the creatures that inhabit our environment," I affirmed.

"Buffalo Feather, you have been an exceptional student and a true friend. You will become a formidable medicine man. As I embark on my journey to the spirit world, remember that it is not something to fear. The spirit world holds immense power and wisdom that you can tap into for guidance. Its manifestations and experiences are the true reality. It is the world from which you and all of humanity originate. You must explore the flow of life between internal and external energies. There is no need to fear what cannot be perceived through your physical senses. Although it is time for me to move on, I will always be with you," Thunder Dog reassured me.

"I will deeply miss you, my teacher," I expressed, my voice choked with anguish.

"It is alright to shed tears. We will weep together," he said, tears streaming down his wrinkled face. "Listen closely as I share these profound words. I will impart to you a message about death. These words, written by a spiritual being, contain great truths and insights. They will hold a special meaning for you. At this point in your journey, you may encounter numerous unanswered questions about death and the afterlife."

"The tangible world serves its purpose in providing answers when seeking wisdom about the physical reality. However, you must release the need for tangible proof and allow your spiritual powers to guide you toward a complete understanding. You have spent many years honing your skills and abilities to navigate the material world, and you have done well in developing yourself in that regard. Yet, you must question why you have not equally cultivated your spiritual awareness. You have often pondered other aspects of life such as The Being, The Soul, and God. However, you have not fully integrated those realities into your beliefs," Thunder Dog explained.

"You know that believing in a higher spiritual power is not mere foolish thinking. There is a power that serves as the source of all life, and that life-giving energy flows through each of us. That divine force remains within us long after the physical body has ceased to exist. Therefore, utilize your spiritual awareness to find answers to all your questions. Deep in your heart and being, you know that the one you love will always be with you. Your spiritual energies merge as one with the Divine Creator for eternity. Let your spiritual light guide your path, and have faith in your heart that the soul of your loved one rests in a peaceful place. The two of you will reunite on the other side at the culmination of your respective journeys," Thunder Dog shared.

"I had no idea you read Love Quest! I would never have guessed that you read any of my books," I exclaimed.

"Of course, I have read them all, even the ones you have yet to write. I thought your message on death would aid me in letting go of my body's impending death. All life is in constant motion on the Medicine Wheel. Nothing ends without marking the beginning of something new,"

Thunder Dog said, holding me in a warm embrace. "Remember these teachings, Buffalo Feather." He paused. "Now, it is time to return to the village. I must bid farewell to my friends."

We embraced once more before making our way back to the village. My mind was filled with countless thoughts as I tried to comprehend what Thunder Dog had conveyed. Even in the face of death, he prioritized the Divine Creator and Mother Earth over the concerns of the people, I marveled. We walked in silence for the remainder of the journey, our hearts heavy with love and sorrow.

"Everyone is prepared for your visit," Naomi informed us.

Thunder Dog and I embraced, and then he entered his hut to gather the items he wished to distribute. As he visited each family, he bestowed a gift along with a blessing. Grateful, they thanked him and touched his body one last time to express their appreciation for all he had done and been to them throughout the years.

Before leaving each family, he advised, "Remember, those of you blessed with an abundance of food and possessions must always share with those who are lacking. Let go of attachment to your belongings. May you're giving and receiving be free of any sense of obligation. The Medicine Wheel turns, and tomorrow, those in need may find themselves blessed with abundance, which they, too, can share. I give you my possessions as a reminder to share all that you have. You will always have my spirit to guide you on your journey."

Late into the night, Thunder Dog returned to his hut to rest. Naomi and I also gathered in his hut, engaging in conversation as he slept. The distant sound of the drumbeat continued. Thoughts of his imminent passing consumed my mind.

Finally, Naomi and I attempted to sleep. I tossed and turned until around two in the morning when a powerful energy swept over my body.

"What is happening?" I asked, feeling Thunder Dog's presence hovering over me.

"It is time for me to begin my journey home," he responded. I glanced at Naomi, who was still peacefully asleep.

"It is not yet time for me to go," Thunder Dog clarified. "I didn't wake Naomi because she has already come to terms with my impending death. However, you are still processing the situation. You feel the need to take action. Yet, you have not fully accepted that death is an integral part of the birth and life process. It is not separate from it. Consider this perspective: everyone is constantly undergoing a process of dying and regeneration within their bodies. We could even refer to life as a continuous cycle of reincarnation, where new flesh is created to replace the old. We never possess the same body we were born with. In every moment of our lives, we experience cellular death and rebirth."

"I am now at the final stage, where my cells will no longer regenerate, and my spirit must leave the physical vessel it has inhabited for many years. The good news is that I have not held a strong attachment to my flesh, so I have no fear of death. The truth is, I am not my body. It has served its purpose, but the time has come to release it. My essence is spiritual, eternally linked to the Divine Spirit."

"I have not clung to my body because I have often disconnected vital forces from it. The body can be a great hindrance in the search for truth. While my body is passing away, death signifies freedom, rebirth, and liberation. It is a gateway to infinity and a wondrous opening into eternity. I am embarking on a new spiritual life, made possible only through death."

"I understand, and I am gradually accepting what is. My resistance is dissipating with each passing minute. Farewell, my dear friend," I replied, my voice filled with a mixture of sadness and acceptance.

"Do not attach yourself to the body and mistake it for your spirit. Always remember this: I have departed this world a contented man. Death is the measure of my life. The way I pass on allows me to gauge how I have lived. Travel in peace, my son. You are going to be a remarkable medicine man someday, if you continue your training."

The powerful energy emanating from Thunder Dog's body gently permeated the room. Naomi opened her eyes and sensed the energy.

"I can feel his presence," she said. "He is departing from us now. It is time for prayer and meditation. Open the door so that those who wish to delve deeper into prayer and meditation can participate as his being gradually dissipates into everything and nothingness."

"Why?" I inquired.

"His physical body will release the potent energy it currently holds, allowing it to expand and merge with the divine whole. When this occurs, individuals who are in a peaceful inner state will experience the natural release of light. By allowing this light to pass through your body, you will also experience the essence contained within that light. You may witness Thunder Dog's life and teachings unfold from beginning to end," Naomi explained.

As I opened the door, I noticed people already gathered outside. Naomi arranged the bed with Thunder Dog's body at the center of the room. He was adorned with symbols painted on his face, while his medicine bag, pipe, and tobacco lay nearby. Many eagle feathers adorned his hair.

"Why hadn't I noticed those feathers before?" I pondered.

As people entered, they sat, knelt, prayed, or meditated in silence. The sounds of singing and drumming resonated from outside. The soft melodies of a flute drifted through the door, creating a magical and emotional ambiance.

Holding a rattle made of buffalo hide in one hand and a spirit stick in the other, Naomi walked clockwise around the bed. Occasionally, she closed her eyes. Each time she reached the head of the bed, she shook her rattle and briefly looked at the people in the room, as if searching for someone, before continuing her walk.

The air was filled with the scent of sweet grass and sage. People continued their prayers and soft, gentle singing. The chants seemed to stir a powerful energy. The balance between singing and chanting evoked strong emotions within me, and I found myself sitting on the floor.

Mourning Dove and Canyon approached and sat next to me. Canyon placed his hand on my shoulder for support.

Naomi once again reached the head of the bed. She looked up, and Black Bull stood up, locking eyes with her. He expressed his desire to prolong his mourning by becoming the "spirit keeper." Naomi then cut off a lock of Thunder Dog's hair and handed it to him.

Black Bull wrapped the lock of hair in a sacred felt cloth and left the hut, cradling it in his arms as if it were Thunder Dog's body. Outside, he announced to the tribe that he had taken on the responsibilities of the spirit keeper, and his ceremony would last for one year. He created a spirit bundle by combining the lock of hair with sweet grass and shaded buffalo hair, carefully wrapping them together in a special covering.

Suddenly, a whitish light enveloped Thunder Dog's body, growing in intensity and changing colors. Beams of light, about six inches long, emerged from his aura, propelling themselves through the air. Each beam transformed in color and left a distinct aroma in its wake. Remarkably, as the beams passed through individuals, there was no harm or fear, and they seemed unaffected.

One of the beams approached Canyon and me, and we remained still. The beam entered Canyon, and upon exiting his body, it fragmented into numerous small lights that ascended upwards. As I observed Canyon, a peculiar tingling sensation stirred within my chest. Another beam was on the verge of entering me, accompanied by a voice or whisper infiltrating my mind.

"Life is an everlasting cycle of change. We and our world shall never remain the same. We must always honor Mother Earth and the Divine Creator," the voice echoed.

I glanced at Canyon, seeking confirmation.

"Did you hear that?" I asked him.

"No, I didn't. Each beam carries a different message. Only the person it passes through can hear it. Each beam holds a fragment of Thunder Dog's life, experiences, or teachings," Canyon explained.

The hut became filled with beams of light, interweaving within the bodies of everyone present. Many voices emanated from the beams, but I could only comprehend the words of the ones that entered me. Not only did they convey messages, but they also transmitted emotions, visuals, sounds, tactile sensations, and tastes.

Another beam entered me, and I heard the sound of running water. A second beam entered the center of my forehead, just above my eyes. Before me materialized the waterfall where Thunder Dog was born. This particular beam carried his birth energy, and I observed as his spirit animated his body upon his arrival into the world.

Flocks of birds sang near his father's hut as his mother gave birth to him. A lizard scurried across the ground, encircling his father's pacing form. A bolt of lightning streaked through the sky, followed by the distant rumble of thunder. On a nearby hilltop, a wild dog howled.

The air was imbued with the fragrance of fresh pine, and I heard the rhythmic tapping of grinding corn. Three women ground corn in preparation for the feast commemorating Thunder Dog's birth.

A woman carried baby Thunder Dog to his father, who lifted him high overhead. "Behold my son, who will surpass me. My son and I honor the four directions, Mother Earth, Father Sky, and the Divine Creator. Please guide him on his journey as you have guided me along my path," his father declared.

A majestic brown and white hawk soared gracefully in the sky, riding the currents of wind. Baby Thunder Dog laughed joyously as the hawk circled above, calling out to him. In the distance, rolling hills and a winding river came into view. A vast herd of buffalo meandered along the riverbank, raising a dust cloud that stretched for miles.

Two large grouse scurried across the ground, while a flock of blue jays perched on a tree branch, nearly concealing it entirely. A red-breasted robin and a cardinal danced in a semicircle, emitting soft coos. A double rainbow arched overhead, enveloping Thunder Dog and his father.

Another beam entered me, causing the scene to fade away. A voice spoke, "The Earth is a spiritual presence that demands reverence. We must always strive for balance with Mother Earth. All things are interconnected, and whatever affects one, impacts all."

Surveying the room, I noticed the beams gradually diminishing. After a few more minutes, they had vanished entirely. The energy and emotions I had experienced had drained me completely.

Sensing the dissipation of energy, Naomi tapped her spirit post on the floor, signaling for everyone to depart from the hut swiftly.

"It is time for me to prepare the body," she declared.

"Should I leave?" I inquired.

"No, stay. If you open yourself to awareness, you can still sense his energy dissipating. It will take a considerable amount of time for his energy to completely depart from his body."

Moved by her words, I drew closer to Thunder Dog's body, embracing the final moments of his presence.

"Yes, I can feel it, although it's not as intense," Naomi said.

"Come in, Crazy Deer, and let's get started."

"I have the buffalo skins. They are moist," Crazy Deer said.

They wrapped a skin robe around Thunder Dog's body and bound it tightly with rawhide thongs from head to foot. A second, water-softened robe was wrapped around the body. It also was carefully bound with thongs. Then the body was wrapped with a third robe.

"At last, all the air is gone," Naomi said.

Black Bull led a horse pulling a travois to the entrance of the hut. Someone had painted red blotches on the horse's body. We placed Thunder Dog's body on the travois and Naomi led the horse to the holy burial grounds. Crazy Deer, Black Bull and I followed along behind her. The rest of the tribe walked slowly behind us.

At the site, Black Bull had built a scaffold out of four upright poles. On the top of the poles a number of smaller branches were intertwined to make a raft-like platform to hold the body. It was surprisingly strong. We placed Thunder Dog's body upon it with his feet turned toward the rising sun. Then we tied down his body with rawhide.

With his body above ground there was nothing separating him from the Divine Creator. As his energy left his body, it was free to return where it had come from.

Naomi said a prayer. She raised her spirit pots high in the air and walked back to the village. Some people stayed at the burial site and others went back to their daily routine. Mourning Dove, Canyon, and I sadly walked back to the village.

"We're going to spend some time in the forest together. We both have much work to do in our new quest," Canyon said.

"I must go home," I said. "It's been a long three weeks. It feels like a lifetime has passed."

We embraced and said good-bye. Tears were in our eyes. They picked up their packs and disappeared into the forest.

Naomi stood in the doorway of Thunder Dog's hut. I walked over.

"It's time for me to return to my world," I said.

"I know. We will miss you," she said.

"I will be back soon."

"I know you will."

We embraced and I said good-bye to everyone that passed us on my way to my car. Soon I was on the highway headed home. It felt good to have some time alone to process all that had happened. The native way is a good way to live.

Chapter 8

DANCING MOON

"Welcome, Buffalo Feather," Naomi said as we embraced.

"I can't believe it's been six months since I was here for Canyon's wedding," I said.

"And Thunder Dog's funeral. It's time that you stop mourning." Naomi said.

"I have been withdrawn and detached," I spoke.

"That's why I summoned you for this sweat. It's time to use your powers and be the great medicine man that Thunder Dog taught you to be. Grieving time is over. You have lots of work to do."

I walked with Naomi to the sweat lodge. She began staring into the fire pit.

"What are you doing?" I asked.

"I'm trying to identify the color of the ashes remaining from the last Sweat Lodge. It will tell me what type of sweat this one should be. If the ashes are red, I will lead a healing sweat. If they're yellow, it will be about change on the personal level and new directions. Green calls for physical abundance." She smiled.

I looked into the ashes.

"They look black to me, with just a little red around the edges. If red is for healing, what does black mean?"

"Black calls on a strong spiritual energy used for healing, death and transition. During a black sweat it will get intense as we call on death energy and use its powers to help us transition our lives to the next spiritual level. This is going to be a powerful sweat. I will need Crying Wolf to be the fire tender for this one."

"Why Crying Wolf?"

"His experience will support each of us as we participate. He will ensure that the fire doesn't go out before we are complete. I never want the fire to go out when I am leading a sweat, but I particularly want the fire to stay lit when the ceremony is calling for death and transition.

"I see your point. We do need Crying Wolf."

Naomi sat on the ground with her legs crossed and closed her eyes.

I instinctively knew that she was calling Crying Wolf. After a few minutes she opened her eyes.

"He's on his way. Go tell the others that we are going to have a black sweat and to make more black tobacco ties. They will know what to do. Crying Wolf and I will make more flags when he gets here."

"Okay."

I walked to the waterfall where Lame Deer, Black Fish and Little Turtle were sitting on the ground making ties.

"Naomi wants us to make black ties. It will be a healing, death and transition sweat," I said.

"Are you sure you're ready for a death sweat?" Lame Deer said.

"Black is a powerful sweat," Black Fish said. "The spirits come right up to your face and try to take your life force away. They'll succeed if you don't show great courage and have ties to exchange."

"What are you talking about?" I asked.

"Didn't Naomi tell you that a Death Sweat is very powerful. Your spiritual powers must be strong to participate in a black sweat. This will be a good test of your courage and your commitment to our ways." Little Turtle laughed.

All the talk about spirits taking my life force made me feel concerned. I heard a voice from behind me.

"Buffalo Feather is a powerful medicine man. He's ready for the Death Sweat, and so am I."

I turned and saw Black Hawk.

"What are you doing here?" I asked.

"When Naomi called Crying Wolf to support her, I asked him if I could participate. It will be my first black sweat. I thought it would be great if we experienced it together. Now, let's make more ties before Naomi starts the sweat without us. She will, you know. I brought more cotton cloth and tobacco if we need it."

We began making tobacco ties. Each tie contained a tiny pinch of tobacco bundled inside a small square of black or red colored cloth, looped with cotton string. Every inch or two we placed a loop around the next bundle until we had a string of ties. As we made the prayer ties, we never tied knots, which would have stopped the prayers. Instead, we used loops, which allowed the prayers to flow freely.

"Each color tie has a special meaning," Black Hawk said. "Each invites the spirit of its color into the lodge and asks for blessings from that relation."

"A yellow tie draws on the powers of the great eagle, male energy, and illumination of the East," Lame Deer said.

"Red draws on the energy of the child, the powers of South, faith, trust, innocence, and one or more of the animals of the South Shield," Black Fish said.

"You already know that black represents death and transition. But it also calls on the powers of the West, female energy, the bear, introspection and goals," Little Turtle said.

"White ties signify the North, the elders, gratitude and wisdom. Blue ties carry the energy of Father Sky, the Great Star Nation, and all things above. The green prayer tie contains the energy of Mother Earth, the plant kingdom, and all things green and growing," Black Fish said.

"That's enough ties. It's time to begin the sweat." Crying Wolf smiled as he approached us.

We followed Crying Wolf to the sweat lodge.

Naomi circled the sweat lodge clockwise around the fireplace, trailing particles of tobacco. Then she left a trail from the fireplace to the lodge opening. She entered the lodge with her remaining portion of tobacco and circled the stone pit, lightly sprinkling tobacco. She signaled me to proceed into the lodge.

By now we were undressed and our bodies smudged with sage. I held a clear quartz and amethyst crystal in my hand. Naomi smudged me again. After saying a prayer, I entered the lodge. I placed my crystals on the altar and my ties around my neck. Large black tobacco cloth flags were hanging in each of the four directions.

Black Hawk followed me. One by one, the others entered. When we were all seated around the fire pit, Naomi entered. She sat by the doorway to lead the ceremony. Crying Wolf, the fire tender, dropped the thick blanket flap covering the door opening. Instantly the lodge became black. We were silent, to allow our minds and bodies time to adjust before Crying Wolf passed in the hot glowing stones.

"There will be many powerful energies entering the lodge and you may become frightened, but try to endure," Naomi said. "If you can't endure the spirits, please call out and I will halt the ceremony so you can leave through the doorway."

After a few minutes Naomi asked Crying Wolf to bring the stones. He passed the stones in with an elk horn. After Crying Wolf brought in seven stones, he passed in a rawhide container of water and a wooden cup. Then he closed the flap again.

The lodge was dark and quiet. The red-orange stones glowed within the dome-shaped lodge. Naomi sprinkled something on the hot stones. It quickly filled the lodge and my lungs. I felt a little dizzy and everything around me whirled slowly. I closed my eyes briefly. When I opened them, I saw the image of a lion, a crow and a feather in the hot rocks. The crow turned into a woman with long hair and an infectious smile. She began dancing slowly and her body glowed from the heat. Suddenly she disappeared, leaving me with an unfamiliar feeling of mixed joy and sorrow as I sensed her pain.

In a few short minutes, I saw many images within the red-hot rocks. These images slowly changed as I looked at them. I sensed their intelligence and a timeless awareness of all that has happened throughout eternity. The strange feeling of joy and sorrow faded in and out of my consciousness.

As we stared deeply into the glowing stones, everyone's thoughts and spirits slowly merged.

Naomi poured four cups of water on the stones. Hot steam shot upward, filling the darkened interior of the lodge. We all began sweating profusely. I placed my head between my knees, hoping it would help me endure the intense heat.

"Oh, great spiritual beings, living high in the sky and looking down on this world," Naomi said, "please hear our prayers. We're calling on the powers of the four directions, in our four prayers and our four endurances'."

I was becoming dizzier. While I could see Naomi's mouth moving slowly, I could not make out her sentences. There seemed to be long pauses between each word. "Red... is... the... color... of... the... East...."

She, Thunder Dog's spirit, was honoring the four directions, and the pauses between her words grew longer. I closed my eyes, attempting to withstand the heat and find balance within myself. Suddenly, something tugged on the tobacco tie around my neck. When I opened my eyes, I beheld Thunder Dog's spirit. He took a pinch of tobacco and transferred a surge of powerful energy into me.

"It's time for you to utilize your astral powers to aid a healer who has lost their way. Open your mind and soul, allowing yourself to hear the cry for help. Follow that connection and support them in rediscovering the correct path," Thunder Dog's spirit instructed.

"Who is it? How will I recognize them amidst the other energies?" I asked.

"It's not a 'he'; she is a descendant of Wild Elk, a great Sioux medicine man who belongs to my primary soul cluster. He is often referred to as 'grandfather' due to his age and wisdom. He has requested your assistance; her name is Dancing Moon, and he wants you to join with her on an astral level to help her find her way back to the spiritual path."

"Okay, I understand. I will connect with her on the astral plane," I replied.

"You can connect with her by opening your mind and reaching out to her. You will hear her pain. You will feel her pain. You will recognize her, and she will respond," Thunder Dog's spirit explained.

With an open mind, I began to meditate, forging a connection with the Divine Creator and all that exists. My mind became clear, and amidst the astral plane, I encountered numerous cries for help. As I continued my search, I sensed a consciousness that evoked both joy and sorrow, flickering intermittently in my mind, just like when I witnessed the crow transforming into a woman. The compulsion was too strong to resist. Thunder Dog's voice resounded, "You're on the right path. She needs your wisdom and guidance."

Extending my etheric energy, I connected with the consciousness I had sensed. Our minds engaged in communication.

"I hear your call for help. Join with me, so I may assist you," I conveyed.

"Who are you?" she inquired.

"I am Buffalo Feather, a medicine man sent by your grandfather. Focus your energy on me, so I can transport us to a place free from the thoughts of others," I responded.

"I want to accompany you, but I'm a bit afraid," she replied.

"Alright, we will journey to a sacred place of your creation. You must still focus on me. Simultaneously, hold an image of the Divine Creator and your spiritual sanctuary within your mind. I will know when you have formed that image. Then, using our combined energy, I will transition us to a different dimension, where we will enter the sanctuary you created. Is that agreeable to you?" I reassured her.

"Yes, I'm beginning to meditate now," she confirmed.

Suddenly, I found myself walking along a pathway cutting through a vibrant poppy field. The field teemed with beautiful red, pink, purple, and orange poppies, swaying gracefully in the gentle breeze. Advancing deeper into the field, a soft gust of wind cooled my face and arms. Birds sang joyously, while large butterflies of various sizes, shapes, and colors fluttered gracefully through the air, each dancing above a poppy.

Overhead, clouds resembled remnants of a recent rainstorm, with the sun peeking through sporadically. In the distance, I spotted a structure with an ocean backdrop. Its red, barn-shaped door was discernible, but the color and presence of windows remained elusive. I knew instinctively that this was the sacred sanctuary she had created.

Upon entering the sanctuary, golden light enveloped me from all directions. The light emanated warmth and invited me further. The room was spacious, featuring a fire pit at its center, a shelf along one wall, and a multi-paned window through which light poured. Impulsively, I circled the fire pit three times, intuitively understanding that dancing was the only way to honor the room and the healing light. Unexpectedly, the light permeated me, instantly nourishing my soul.

"Thank you," I expressed my gratitude aloud.

Resting on a shelf, I noticed a rock split perfectly down the middle. Its brown exterior displayed various gradations of color within. An ancient artifact, it held the potent energies of the mineral kingdom. Curiosity prompted me to pick up the rock, instantly experiencing the powerful forces of cohesion, adhesion, and aggregation radiating over me. The energy was so intense that I quickly set the rock down and took a step back. Closing my eyes, I grounded myself and, after a few minutes, regained balance with the mineral kingdom.

"Thank you for your energy. I honor the powers of the mineral kingdom," I conveyed.

As I continued to survey the room, I observed rough timber comprising the walls and ceiling, while wide strips of pine formed the floor. The room exuded a sense of size, power, freedom, and openness. The air carried the refreshing scent of pine and wild sage.

The energy of another person filled the room, a familiar energy. I saw a woman looking at me with a smile, realizing that she was the same person whose image I had seen in the hot stones.

"Are you one of my guides? Are you the one who called me here?" she asked.

"Yes, I am. I have many messages for you. But first, do you know where you are?" I replied.

"Yes, I do. We are in my sanctuary. You helped me create this wonderful place when I felt your mind in communication with me. You instructed me to meditate, saying that I would receive guidance and direction from my higher self and the Divine Creator. However, I didn't expect to see you here so soon. I had barely finished exploring all the rooms when you arrived."

"I am here because of your strong desire to return to the spiritual path. Don't be alarmed," I reassured her.

"I am not alarmed, just surprised. You must know Grandfather. I encountered him in one of the other sanctuary rooms. Your energy feels like his, although he never spoke," she shared.

"You mean he never used words. Grandfather is always communicating with you. He is attempting to teach you how to communicate in silence, without the constant chatter of the mind, and from a place where you remain connected to the Divine Creator," I explained.

"Because he wouldn't speak, I completely missed his message. I must open my awareness to communicate with my heart and not rely solely on words," she realized.

"As you continue to pray, meditate, and visit your sanctuary, your fear will diminish, and your heart will open further to share love. Love will become the driving force behind your communication. It will be your intention, and your connection with everyone and everything will expand. Allow this knowledge to permeate your being," I encouraged her.

"I am so excited, but let me show you the rest of the sanctuary. Perhaps you can help me understand more about the elements within my sacred home," she suggested.

We proceeded into other rooms branching off from the main room. I followed her into an empty room, which had nothing in it except for a large eagle's feather resting in the center of the floor.

The presence of the feather imbued the room with a distinct ambiance, contrasting with the previous room with the rock. The ceiling reached about 12 feet high, adorned with a large modern window overlooking a grassy field and numerous tall evergreen trees.

Returning my attention to the feather, I felt the energies of sensation, attraction, and repulsion, the three forces of the Animal and Plant

Kingdom resonating within me. The woman picked up the feather and looked at me.

"You've already met Rock. This is Feather," she introduced.

"Hello Feather. I am Buffalo Feather. I am here to support Dancing Moon in discovering her purpose," I acknowledged, addressing the feather.

"Are you here to teach me more about myself?" she asked.

"Yes, I am. But it's all here within your sanctuary. You have done an excellent job of tapping into the Divine Creator's energy to create the perfect space for receiving guidance on your higher self. You simply need some assistance to get started," I assured her.

"I know that this place is special," she acknowledged. "But I need to comprehend everything that is here. Despite my success in the business world, I feel unsatisfied because I sense that I am not progressing towards my divine purpose. I am uncertain about what that purpose is."

"Let's continue our walk. I am here to support you in any way I can," I offered.

We moved on to another room, where an elderly woman sat on the floor.

"This is Grandmother. She is a strong spiritual guide, but I struggle to understand her messages," the woman explained.

"Is it that you don't understand or is it that you don't follow her guidance? You have requested the revelation of your higher purpose, but your mind is reluctant to release its attachment to the world and live from spirit. I am here to show you the pathway, but I cannot compel you to follow it. Ultimately, the choice of your path rests with you through your actions. Free choice will always be yours, for it is a gift that the Divine Creator will never take away," I emphasized.

Dancing Moon's face appeared saddened by the realization.

I looked at her with a smile and spoke, "You have a special gift to share with the world, and you possess the ability to share it. I will be by your side, guiding you just as Thunder Dog, my teacher, did for me. It is an honor for me to teach you everything I know. However, remember that your accountability is much greater than someone who is unaware of this path. Now, let me acknowledge Grandmother."

Turning to the old lady on the floor, I greeted her, "Hi, Grandmother. I am deeply honored to be in your presence." Grandmother responded with a warm smile, her large black eyes radiating deep love for all.

"You must understand that Grandmother and Grandfather represent expressions of the human kingdom," I explained to Dancing Moon. "They are always attempting to teach you how to transcend the conditioned ego mind and utilize your free will to live from the spirit. Within your sanctuary, you have the four primary forces that influence all manifestations. Each of the four physical kingdoms - mineral, plant, animal, and human - possesses an essential quality of power that governs it and is associated primarily with an element. This unique energetic balance will aid in teaching you about spiritualism and manifestation."

We entered a vast room with ceilings reaching over 50 feet high. One wall was entirely made of glass, stretching from floor to ceiling, providing a breathtaking view of the ocean. The waves gently moved during high tide. Hieroglyphics, pictographs, and various symbols adorned the other three walls, emanating ancient wisdom. In the center of the room, on a small table, sat a large book resembling a journal, accompanied by a golden pen. I opened the book to the first page, only to find it blank. Leafing through the pages, I discovered that every page was devoid of writing.

"You haven't written in your journal. This book is here for you to document your learnings and share them with the world. This room contains the history of mankind, allowing you to see the diverse paths humanity has traversed. This knowledge can support you in fulfilling your purpose," I explained.

Dancing Moon asked, "Is this my Purpose Room?"

"You can call it that if you prefer, but the entire sanctuary is here to teach you how to live from your higher self and fulfill your purpose," I answered.

"Do you know my purpose? Sometimes I get a sense of it, but I haven't been able to see it clearly," she expressed.

"Yes, I know your purpose, and so do you. Don't get caught in your mind's trap. Don't allow your thinking mind to make you believe that you don't know your purpose. Right now, relax and open yourself to receive loving communication from the Divine Creator. Close your eyes, focus on your purpose, and your sacred journal. Now, ask the Divine Creator any question you desire," I instructed.

"I want to know my purpose. Divine Creator, what is my purpose?" Dancing Moon spoke aloud.

"Did you hear the Divine Creator? He answered you," I pointed out.

"I heard something, but I couldn't discern the words or their meaning," Dancing Moon responded.

"The Divine Creator has revealed your purpose to you. He also mentioned that the answer to each question you pose will be automatically written in your journal. The journal is here for you to record all your conversations with the Divine Creator, for sharing with the world. Until now, you haven't asked any questions. That's why the pages are blank."

Dancing Moon rushed to the journal, opened it, and began writing. After a few minutes, she stopped and read aloud what she had written. "Your purpose is to teach, heal, and guide. Your focus will be on assisting people in healing their emotional wounds, which will also address many physical issues. You are destined to aid the world in healing the emotional pain stemming from conflicts among the four different worlds: red, yellow, black, and white. You have a powerful role in unifying all tribes and bringing harmony to all kingdoms."

"You must visit this room frequently and record your insights. It will help you fulfill your purpose," I advised.

"This room frightens me a little," Dancing Moon confessed. "I don't think I want to understand the hieroglyphic messages. I can never decipher the symbols."

"Don't be afraid. The symbols hold information that can assist you. Some of the information may be unsettling, but that has been humanity's history until now. Humanity does not have to remain on the same path. Each of us possesses free will. We can change whenever we genuinely desire it. We must change soon, as the spiritual energy on this planet is shifting to a higher level of vibration. As the world ascends, anything not vibrating at the same frequency will be dismantled. I hold great hope that humanity will change in time. Now, hold a question in your mind and read one of the symbols. You will see that the process will not harm you," I assured her.

"Wait just a minute. I'm not ready to read a hieroglyphic, a sacred symbol or whatever you call them. I'm still not sure about talking to the Divine Creator. Let me try asking him another question." Dancing Moon said.

"Okay. Don't let me move you along too fast," I said.

"Although it looks like you're moving slowly, you're giving me more insights than I can handle. When I first experienced you, I thought that your energy was too slow. My energy moves so fast that I felt as if I had to reduce my speed to communicate with you. But now I realize that you're providing so much that I can't keep up with you. I find myself asking you to go slower. That surprises me."

"Things are not always what they appear to be," I said. "You can ask your question whenever you're ready. It's okay for you to need more proof at this stage of your development. At some point, you'll move beyond it. First you must develop faith in the Divine Creator and in your own powers."

"My question is, how can I stay focused on my purpose and live from higher self with all the things that are going on in my daily life?" Dancing Moon opened the journal and wrote, then read it aloud again. "Your mind finds it difficult to stay focused on your purpose, but your spirit does not. Therefore, the more you operate from your spiritual self, the easier it will be to manifest your purpose. Always remember that the world needs your special gift, which is your light. Your guides have been giving you direction, but you have not been listening. That's why Grandfather called Buffalo Feather to help you. You feel that you have lots to do in what you call the real world, but you must not let the physical world stop you from living spiritually."

She looked at me. "It worked." Dancing Moon was silent for a long time.

I broke the silence by asking, "What do you think about the information in your journal?"

"I try to live spiritually most of the time. I know I should live from spirit, but something always gets in the way. Can you help?"

"Yes, if you're ready to make some changes. You seem to have issues with responsibility, time and obligation. You must search your heart and release any negative energy surrounding these areas."

"You hit the nail on the head," she said. "I feel responsible for my family and a small group of friends. They take up time—time that I just don't have. I have a strong sense of obligation to do activities that I put ahead of my spiritual work. Making a living is necessary and it takes up a lot of time and energy. There doesn't seem to be much room for being spiritual."

"Each moment, the purpose of my visit with you is becoming clearer," I said. "You have the ability to be a great teacher, healer and guide. The challenge that you're facing is the same one that many others have faced. Don't turn your back on your divine gift. Instead, choose to integrate your spiritual teaching and healing into your daily life. The work place provides an excellent opportunity to share your teaching with everyone you encounter. Remember, living spiritually has nothing to do with where you are or what work you're doing. Living from spirit is a matter of extending your love to all and not withholding it."

"Tell me again what drew you to me?" Dancing Moon said.

"You're a descendant of Wild Elk, a great Sioux medicine man and spiritual guide. You call him Grandfather. He is from the same soul cluster as Thunder Dog, my old teacher. Even as we speak, I can feel Thunder Dog's powerful spiritual energy all around your sanctuary. He is why I'm here. The Divine Creator directed him to train me as a medicine man so I would fulfill my purpose to teach, heal and guide."

"I do need your help," Dancing Moon said.

"You must visit your sanctuary and meditate each day. It will allow you to remain in communication with the Divine Creator and support you in living in harmony with all. You must touch Mother Earth each day and allow her to nourish your soul. Know, in your heart, that all things are connected through the Divine Spirit and Mother Earth."

"You have many powerful guides but you must listen to them and keep their wisdom in your heart," I said. "You're truly blessed to have Grandmother and Grandfather as your spiritual guides. Their perception of reality is different from yours. Your perceptions are conditioned by the age in which you live. You live in the age of science, which places a great deal of importance on the investigation of matter. On the other hand, Grandmother and Grandfather know that what is seen has its source in the unseen -- the spirit. Therefore, they can teach you much about the true source beyond all physical creation."

"As you embrace their guidance, you will fulfill your purpose to teach, heal, and guide," I assured her. "The Divine Creator holds each of us spiritually accountable for bringing our light to the planet. Now that you have a clear vision of your path, it is essential to take the necessary actions to live a spiritual life. Your guides, along with myself, are here to support you. From this moment onward, our spiritual connection is eternal, so you can call on me and your guides to support you at any time."

Dancing Moon expressed, "This is a lot for me to process right now. I have always felt a strong connection to my native culture and the spiritual path. In the past, many native images have appeared to me in my dreams, both while awake and asleep. But now that I know my path and how to use my sanctuary, I will return to it often to help me stay on the right path and fulfill my purpose," she stated confidently.

Chapter 9

SPIRIT KEEPERS

"Will you tell me more about my native powers, if I have any?" Dancing Moon asked.

"You have many native powers to draw on," I said.

"What are they?"

"You have the powers of the Four Directions or the Four Spirit Keepers," I said.

"What are Spirit Keepers?" she said.

"The Four Spirit Keepers are the caretakers of the universe. They are associated with the four directions: East, South, West, and North. Spirit Keepers are helpers of the Divine Creator, and they are the spiritual forces that keep the universe in existence. They reveal themselves through the language of symbolism, through an individual's inner experience, and sometimes through visions or dreams.

"You need not fear Spirit Keepers. Instead, strive to develop a close and harmonious relationship with them. Each Spirit Keeper has a particular animal or bird that demonstrates some characteristics or qualities that relate the unseen powers to reality. These animals or birds are called Totems.

"Totems offer the Spirit Keepers a way of linking the nonphysical power to a physical symbolic sensor that serves as a connector between different levels of being and different levels of the mind. This is true whether the subject is human, animal, vegetable, mineral, or celestial, and whether the mind level is unconscious, subconscious, conscious, or super-conscious. Because Totems express the qualities of something that is 'alive,' they are more powerful symbols than geometric abstracts. Totems are not Gods, but they are helpers and special messengers. They help us understand the invisible reality behind the representation."

"What are the powers of the Spirit Keepers?" Dancing Moon asked.

"The power of the East is illumination, which opens your spiritual eye and brings enlightenment and discernment. It is the power of new beginnings, fresh new life, and awakening. It's like the rising of dawn whose light replaces darkness and dispels ignorance. If you get up early enough to listen to the start of the dawn and to hear the birds and animals as the sun rises in the east, you will experience the power of the East. You will know the power of enlightenment."

"The Totem animal of the East is the eagle. The eagle is symbolic of the desire to draw closer to the Divine Creator and our higher self. The color of the East is yellow -- the color of the rising sun, illumination, and enlightenment. You can call on the powers of the East to help you seek enlightenment, new beginnings, or a fresh start."

"You can invoke the powers of the East as you perform your morning meditation or when you pray for help to support you in living life from your higher self. The Spirit Keeper of the East will send you divine energy that will support you throughout the day as you encounter issues that take you off track. When you start a new project or activity, East energy will free you of any past negativity that may interfere with your success. I use the powers of the East to help me transition to new levels of consciousness and spirituality."

"Will you help me start using the powers of the East?" Dancing Moon asked.

"Yes, let's meditate now. Sit on the ground and close your eyes. We are one, and our minds and souls are connected with the Divine Creator and all there is. Try to relax. Follow my energy and repeat my words in your mind and feel them within your heart.

"Oh, great Spirit Keeper of the East, I am speaking to you for Dancing Moon. She is learning to speak the words that are in her heart.

"Oh, great Spirit Keeper of the East, please help me as I begin this new phase of my journey to purpose and enlightenment. Support me in fulfilling my divine purpose. I have been chosen by the Divine Creator to teach, heal, and guide. Allow me to awaken so that I may use my special gifts to achieve my purpose. As I walk this earthly plane, give me the spiritual energy to experience the newness of life each moment. Keep me always in the light and disperse the darkness.

"Today my path is clear, and my spiritual eye is open. Allow my spiritual eye to remain open, and my heart to be filled with love for all as I seek the fulfillment of my divine purpose. Please give me the power to stay on the spiritual path and ensure that my pathway is illuminated by your loving spirit. Walking the spiritual path is new for me; I will need your help and guidance along the journey. Please share your energy with me so that I will always choose the path of Higher Light and Higher Self. Thank you, Divine Creator and Spirit Keeper of the East, for sharing your love and powerful energy with me."

We sat in silence. After a few minutes, a large eagle flew into the room. As we watched, the eagle transformed into a beam of yellow light, filling the room. The light surrounded Dancing Moon and became more intense as she tried to speak.

A voice from the light said, "Don't speak, my daughter. I know what is in your heart. I can feel your true love for all. Because your heart is pure and you have great faith, I'm granting you the powers of the East to support you along your journey. Your purpose is clear and will remain so as long as you continue to seek the light within.

"With my powers, you have the ability to see into the darkness and to discern what others cannot see. You can perceive what is hidden by the mind but is visible to the heart. Use these powers wisely and let the manifestation of your gift be experienced daily by all. Remember always that your essence is love and spirituality. They are what you use to heal and where you are guiding others. I am always with you because that is the way of the spirit."

As the glow of the light got brighter, it entered Dancing Moon's solar plexus. The light vanished within her, but her aura continued to glow a brilliant yellow. She looked just like the rising sun early in the morning.

The air smelled of fresh roses. I looked around the room as yellow roses appeared from nowhere, completely surrounding us. A lot of tobacco, deep blue rosemary, and 15-foot-tall wild American ginseng were mixed with the roses.

"I feel alive with insight and healing energy," Dancing Moon said.

"Now that you know how to call on the powers of the East, you can have that feeling anytime you desire," I said with a smile.

Slowly, the yellow glow disappeared as the roses, tobacco, rosemary, and ginseng vanished. We sat in silence, enjoying the energy of the East as it faded and integrated within us. After a few minutes, the air smelled of apple sage.

"I must write the words you spoke for me in the journal," Dancing Moon said.

"They are your words, not mine. I just spoke what I saw in your heart. Speaking with one's heart always pleases the Spirit Keepers," I said.

"What were all those roses?" she asked.

"Flowers enhance the atmosphere and please the senses because their vibration is food for the spirit. Flowers, especially roses, have a strong association with love. It means that roses are a powerful totem plant that you can use to help you stay on your spiritual path. Each person has plants that speak to them. Roses are some of yours." I spoke.

"I'm not all that crazy about roses. They seem so cosmetic and commercial," Dancing Moon said.

"Roses are from the plant kingdom and draw on very powerful energy. Flowers represent the perfection of the cycle of birth, change, and death. The seed is the result of a flower's death -- a death that leaves an impression to carry on as the seed contains the memory of the spark of creation. The essential purpose of plants is to express a thought in the mind of the divine spirit in one place. They do not move but express the qualities of the place where they are.

"Do not allow what man has done to stop you from using roses as a powerful plant totem. It's your choice if you decide not to use them. The East has also given you the powers of tobacco, rosemary, and ginseng as totems. It's your option to use any or all of these plants." I explained.

"Okay, I didn't say I wouldn't use them." Dancing Moon smiled as she hurried to her journal and began writing. After a few minutes, she put her pen down and returned to where I was sitting with a pleased look on her face.

"What about the South? Let's call the Spirit Keeper of the South," Dancing Moon said excitedly.

"The power of the South is for rapid growth, exploration, experimentation, and investigation. The power of the South is for blossoming and unfolding as one's purpose becomes clear. It is the endowment that guides and matures us. It is also the power of trust, and it helps us to trust. The power is like the natural trust of a child in natural and cosmic laws. Whenever you enjoy the things of the earth that grow to full blossom, you are experiencing the power of the South.

"The totem of the South is the mouse. The mouse may appear to be a small and insignificant creature, but its ability to perceive things through touch makes it special. The mouse helps us understand our feelings and emotions and stresses the importance of not confusing power with size. The South's color is red -- the color of our vital energy and lifeblood. You can use the powers of the South for spiritual growth and development. It will also support you in learning the lessons of change."

"Can we call on the Spirit Keeper of the South?" Dancing Moon asked.

"Why don't you try calling the Spirit Keeper this time? Each of us has our own prayers within. I will pray with you. You have to start sometime, why not now?"

"I will," Dancing Moon said.

We faced each other in silence and closed our eyes.

"Oh, great Spirit Keeper of the South. I am praying to ask that I may use your powers to help achieve my purpose. Your powers of exploring and finding out will greatly assist me. Your energy can guide me to the path of highest growth where my spiritual light will shine. Help me trust my feelings and intuition. I have intense passion, but I need your love and wisdom to help me focus so that I may live from my higher self. I know some of the natural and cosmic laws, but I need your help to trust them and make them an important part of my life.

"Let me be like the mouse and perceive things clearly and experience my deep emotions from a spiritual place. Please give me the courage to learn the lessons of life and to develop into the teacher, healer, and guide that is needed to bring light into the world. Let your great power protect me as I continue my journey so that I may fulfill my purpose." Dancing Moon pleaded with great sincerity.

"Very good. Your heart was open," I said.

We opened our eyes and sat in silence. The air again smelled of roses. A small mouse entered the room and transformed into a beam of red light that gradually filled the room. The red energy created a powerful field that surrounded Dancing Moon's body.

A voice from the energy said, "I am the Spirit Keeper of the South. I hear your plea and understand your desire to stay on the spiritual path. You have many lessons to learn. Each will require you to make changes. Your courage has been tested many times, but you haven't learned the lesson. Learning is much more than understanding -- it is a sensitivity that leads to wisdom.

If your experience doesn't change the way you think, you haven't learned anything. You are a spiritual being who has an earthly purpose to fulfill.

"Right now, your heart is open and you must keep it open. It is easy to be spiritual in this sacred place you have developed with the help of Buffalo Feather and the rest of your guides. It will be beneficial if you listen to their wisdom and implement what they tell you. I will give you some of my powers, not as a test, but as a show of my faith in you. As your commitment to walk the spiritual path grows, the greater your

Southern powers will become. You must continue to pray and meditate so your powers will grow strong."

The red light around Dancing Moon entered the base of her spine. Her aura became bright red as her vital energy increased.

Once again, roses surrounded us. This time, however, they were all red. Also, there was sagebrush, borage, comfrey, and Hawthorne mixed with the roses.

The red glow left the room and we sat in silence, experiencing the energy of the South integrating into us. After a few minutes, Dancing Moon said, "He was very hard on me."

Instantly I responded, "I don't think so. You must remember that the more you know about walking the spiritual path, the greater your accountability is. The Spirit Keeper of the South was letting you know that you have great powers and a responsibility to teach, heal, and guide others in the ways of the light.

You determine the quality of your experience. If you think he was hard, you're right. If you think he wasn't, you're also right. The real question is, what will you choose to do with the powers and the messages you have received."

"I had better write what happened and how I feel about it in my journal. My journal will be one way to teach others. If I keep writing in the journal and sharing it, it will move me toward the fulfillment of my purpose. That's easy enough." Dancing Moon hurried to her journal, opened it, and began writing.

"Although it's easy to commit to doing something at the moment, time has a way of weakening our commitment," I said. "If you call on the powers of the East and South to help you, keeping your journal will be easy."

Dancing Moon nodded her head and went back to writing. After a few minutes, she stopped writing and walked over to me and took a seat. "How long have we been here?" she asked.

Instantly, I felt her energy start to slip away. Her body began to disappear.

"Dancing Moon! Refocus your mind back to your sanctuary. Do not allow your ego mind to pull you away by distracting you with thoughts of time. You must stay here and complete the initial training. Otherwise, it will be much more difficult to start the next time."

Dancing Moon's energy slowly returned to the sanctuary, and her astral body materialized.

"What happened? What did I do?" she asked.

"You went unconscious for a moment. You allowed your ego mind to start worrying about time and the future. You slipped out of the astral plane. One way that you get yourself off track is by worrying about time and what could happen, instead of remaining focused on living spiritually in the moment. You must not allow yourself to fall asleep. If you do, you must quickly return to the present moment, exactly as you just did."

"I don't know if I would have returned so quickly if you hadn't been here to awaken me," Dancing Moon said.

"That's why you must pray and meditate each day. The daily practice of meditation will ensure that you have an opportunity to awaken if you fall asleep and don't know it. Many times, we fall asleep and get so deep in our dreams that we don't know we're dreaming. We think we're in the real world, but we're actually lost in the unreal one."

"I guess you better tell me about the powers of the West," Dancing Moon said.

"The West has wonderful powers that provide strength and introspection. Its powers help you look deep within so you can evaluate the lessons needed for growth and achieve the realization which leads to development. It also gives you the power for self-examination and transformation of your physical experiences into spiritual realities. When you watch while the sun dips slowly below the horizon, you are experiencing the powers of the West. The totem of the West is the grizzly bear, the strongest and fiercest of the bears. It's also the most thoughtful about its decisions. The color of the West is black. Black is the essence from which all form comes.

"You can call on the powers of the West when you seek transformation or evaluation and when you prepare for new action," I said.

"Close your eyes as I call on the West," Dancing Moon said.

"Okay."

"Oh, great Spirit Keeper of the West, I honor you and your unique powers. I know that you have sent me many signs and messages in the past which I didn't heed, but I will heed them now. I'm ready to accept my special gift and my divine purpose. I'm accountable for walking the spiritual path and listening to my guides. They are a great blessing and a wonderful source of support.

"With an open heart, I ask for some of your special powers so that I can achieve my purpose by walking the path of most light. Your energy will help me prepare for the new actions that I must take to achieve my purpose. Please let me be like the great grizzly bear and make wise decisions. Give me the power to be patient and to make the best choices—choices that will keep me on the quest for purpose and enlightenment. Thank you for listening to me."

We sat in silence. Within a few minutes, a big, ferocious grizzly bear entered the room. Dancing Moon shifted slightly to make way for him.

The bear approached her and transformed into a beam of white light with black spots. The light surrounded her.

"Dancing Moon, I am the Spirit Keeper of the West. You can have some of my power to help you on your journey. On the road ahead, you will need my powers as you seek transformation and spiritual enlightenment. You will be confronted with many decisions as you prepare and take new action. In these critical times, drawing on my unique powers will make it easier to use your free will correctly. Always remember that you are my daughter, and I am with you forever. Let my love fill your heart and guide your direction."

The room smelled of fresh roses. Wild rose bushes were everywhere. There were also olives, chamomiles, nettles, and a few small cedar trees mixed with the roses. The energy surrounded Dancing Moon and entered her body through her throat.

Slowly, the white and black glow disappeared, as did the plants. We sat in silence, enjoying the energy of the West as it integrated within us. After a few minutes, the air smelled of thistles.

Dancing Moon rushed to her journal and began writing.

When she finished, she said excitedly, "Let's do the North."

"The power of the North is used to renew and quicken the spirit. It is the power of winter when outwardly nothing appears to be growing, but inwardly Mother Earth is gathering her energies for the new life that is coming. It is also for compassion, concentration, clarity of intent, and purity. However, purity is not the same as self-righteousness.

The totem of the North is the buffalo, which is much like the spirit that gives totally of itself in order to sustain all that exists. White is the color of the North because white is the sum of all colors, and it is regarded as the color of perfection. You can call on the powers of the

North when you are working for the perfection of any endeavor. The power will help you gain strength of will and clarify your intentions."

"I'm ready to meditate," Dancing Moon said.

We closed our eyes.

"Oh, great Spirit Keeper of the North, please share with me your special powers so that I may continue my journey toward purpose and enlightenment. Support me in renewing and quickening my divine spirit. My vision is clear, and I desire to teach, heal, and guide. Allow me to awaken so that I may use my special gifts to achieve my purpose. As I walk this earthly plane, please give me the spiritual energy to experience the newness of life each moment. Keep me always in the light and disperse the darkness.

"Today my course is clear, and my spiritual eye is open. Please allow it to remain open and fill my heart with love for all as I seek the fulfillment of my divine purpose. Give me some of your power so that I may strive for perfection in teaching, healing, and guiding. I will need your help and direction along the journey. Share your energy with me so that I will have strength of will and clarity of intent. Thank you, great Spirit Keeper."

We sat in silence. Soon a large buffalo entered, then transformed into a beam of white light that completely filled the room. The light surrounded Dancing Moon and became more intense as it began whirling around her.

A voice from the light said, "My daughter, I know what is in your soul and heart. I feel your true love for all of humanity. Your heart is becoming purer, and your faith is growing. I grant you my powers to support you along your journey. Keep your purpose clear in your mind and heart. With my powers, you have the ability to renew yourself and keep your heart pure after facing difficult challenges. You have a great journey ahead, and I will be with you every step of the way. I am always with you because that is the way of the spirit."

The glow of the light got brighter and entered the top of Dancing Moon's head. It vanished within her, but her aura glowed a brilliant white.

The scent of fresh roses filled the air. A quick look around the room revealed white roses everywhere. There was sweet grass, red clovers, mullein, and echinacea nestled in the rose bushes.

"I'm so energized," Dancing Moon said.

Gradually, the white glow disappeared as the plants vanished. We remained in silence and enjoyed the energy of the North integrated within us. After a few minutes, the air smelled of dandelions.

Dancing Moon wrote in her journal as I sat in silent meditation. When she stopped writing, we looked at each other and smiled.

"Thank you," she said. "I'm most grateful for your kindness and the great gifts you helped bring to me. The beautiful experience with the Spirit Keepers has expanded me in so many ways. I am glad to have found you and created this wonderful new spiritual home."

"I am honored to help. It is my purpose, and I will always be here to support you," I said.

Chapter 10

BUTTERFLY CLAN

"Do I have any more powers?" Dancing Moon asked.

"Yes. Did you notice the butterflies as you walked to your sanctuary?"

"Yes, the sky and the poppies were filled with them. I've never seen so many colorful butterflies. It was breathtaking."

"Your sanctuary extends beyond these walls and this structure. It includes everything that was on the path to the building. The surroundings are powerful totems for you and you can draw on their spiritual energies," I said.

"What do butterflies mean?"

"It means that you are of the Butterfly Clan. The butterfly is extraordinary because it begins life as a crawler. Later, through a process of transformation, it learns to fly. Its wings are the color of the rainbow, which gives it wonderful healing abilities. With the butterfly as your totem for elemental air, you can transform and stay in perpetual activity. The butterfly also transforms whatever it touches with its beauty. You are one of the butterfly people, which gives you the power to be a great transformer and a strong influencer.

"You will feel at home when you are active, enjoying a variety of new places, new ideas, new things to do and new ways of doing them. You prefer to be quick and lively; you feel like you always need to be busy, never wanting to stay still too long. You have an affinity with air, so you will be invigorated by being out in the open and away from confinement of any kind."

"Many of the characteristics are just like me," Dancing Moon said. "Some of them create problems though."

"Remember, each totem gives you powers that you can use. You still will have to use free will to apply them effectively. For example, the ability to stay in perpetual activity supports you in doing lots of things. However, if you stay active but don't work on the right things, or if you don't stay focused on one thing long enough to complete it, you will waste energy and avoid making a difference. The right action and focus are required to bring your gifts to the world."

"I do feel that I waste time and it drives me crazy," Dancing Moon said. "I feel that I have so much to do and not enough time to do it."

"You believe that time exists and you also believe that you have too much to do. But that's not actually the case. In reality, you have too much time and not enough to do. As you are eternal, there is only one thing to do -- extend your love by living your life from spirit. I know this isn't the thinking that forms the context of how you live your life. However, if you set up your human experience in this way, you easily win the game of life. Winning the game of life consists of being happy, fulfilled, making a contribution to others, being loving and spiritual.

"You must stop trying to live your life with time-bounded awareness. It's too limiting. This limited reality results in the ego being fully engaged, because the ego exists only in time. A time-based reality also creates the illusion that you are separated from others and from the Divine Creator. It blocks the flow of your spiritual awareness.

"You can expand or create time if you remain connected to your spiritual self. Time is a big illusion. It is not fixed. For the human experience, time is a useful tool. It helps you become aware of what is important. It can be an effective training tool to support you in choosing what is important -- living from your higher self and spiritual teaching. When you believe that you don't have enough time, you have given time the power to control your life and block your spiritual growth and development.

"The real purpose of time is to enable you to learn how to use your life constructively. Time will cease for you when it's no longer useful in facilitating your learning. When you are living from spirit and love, the need for a time-bounded reality will continually decease, until it disappears because it is no longer necessary. In this sense, love is timeless because it has nothing to do with time at all. Love doesn't live in time. It is eternal."

"I must remember that time is an illusion," Dancing Moon said. "I know air is an element. Are there others?"

"You have air, fire, water and earth. Your life on this earth began when you took that first breath of air at birth. The inhalation of air brings expansion and expression through the element of fire, which enabled your spirit to activate your mind and express itself through personality. Your emotions express the way you feel about what you perceive, and they flow like elemental water. Elemental earth finds expression in your practical actions and regards for material realities. So, the way you live and conduct your life is an expression of the energies flowing through you.

"Each of the four directions has an element. The East element is fire, representing the direction of determination. South's element is water, symbolizing the direction of giving. The West's element is earth, associated with the direction of holding. North's element is air, representing the direction of receiving.

Air can be likened to mental energy, encompassing ideas and ephemeral thoughts that arise suddenly and vanish quickly without being seen. Fire is the energy of light emitted by the sun, sharing qualities with the light of the spirit—spiritual illumination and enlightenment. Water possesses characteristics of fluidity and motion. The element of water can be compared to emotions and feelings, representing energies in a fluid state. Earth embodies inertia, stability, and solidity. Thus, elemental earth in the West possesses qualities similar to material objects and the physical body."

"That's a lot to remember," Dancing Moon said.

"You just need to remember to live from spirit and love. The rest will be there when you need it. I sense some areas where you have interchanged the forces of the South and the West, resulting in holding onto your emotions and giving with your body. Additionally, your North and East are a little off balance. You are relying too much on your mind for determination and receiving through the spirit. Sometimes, when you feel fatigued, out of balance, or in pain, it is because these energies are reciprocal.

"You are holding onto your emotions and locking up your heart. Sometimes, you are afraid to express your emotions because you think you're making yourself vulnerable. You believe it is better to convey your feelings through physical things. However, do not let the expression of your love become solely physical. The most genuine expression of love is the giving of oneself and desiring the happiness of a loved one without any strings or conditions.

"By determining with your mind, you act based on logic, primarily focusing on external appearances. Your mind decides what is deemed appropriate to achieve the desired results, often disregarding the possible consequences for others and the environment. You might achieve material results, but your actions or reactions can block the spiritual flow.

"Your principles and ethics are expressions of the spirit, related to intent and will. Rules and laws, on the other hand, are products of the mind. The mind creates laws as an attempt to establish safeguards. Spiritual principles and ethics should underlie everything you are.

"The elements are the building blocks of the physical world, without which there would be no material universe. In the human experience, you perceive and interact with the physical world through your five senses. It is possible to be alive and not see, hear, feel, taste, or smell. However, if you were to lose all five senses, you would know nothing of physical existence," I explained.

"Let me make sure that I have this right," Dancing Moon said. "The most balanced way to use my energies is to first determine with the spirit, second receive with the mind, third give with the emotions, and fourth hold with the body."

After Dancing Moon finished speaking, I said, "I think you understand the elements well. However, let me make sure you are aware that you can also call upon the powers of the butterfly. Sometimes, when you're walking through the poppy field towards your sanctuary, take a moment to stop and meditate. During your meditation, choose a butterfly and focus on it as your mantra. This will create a soothing melody in your mind as the ego dissolves into nothingness. Allow the stillness to open your mind to the transformative powers of the spirit."

"I didn't realize I could tap into the energy of the butterflies," Dancing Moon said.

"You can also utilize the power of the red door in your sanctuary. Red is the color of abundance. A red door opens the pathway to tremendous abundance, prosperity, and wealth. Simply sit and meditate or focus on your door when you seek answers regarding abundance, and listen for its communication. You will be surprised by the results."

"It seems that whatever my problem, praying and meditating in my sanctuary will help," Dancing Moon said. "Now I understand that my sanctuary encompasses both the physical structure and the external environment. It is a sacred place full of powerful energy. I will utilize all of it to stay on the spiritual pathway."

"You have done an excellent job creating a place that supports you on your journey. Are you ready to read some symbols? You don't have to do it now if you don't feel prepared."

"If you know anything about me at all, you know that I love a challenge. I think I'm ready to read a symbol. As they say, the writing is on the wall." She smiled and walked over to the wall, and I followed behind her, smiling as I contemplated the great progress she had made.

"I'll try that one," Dancing Moon said, pointing to a symbol on the wall. It was a small wavy line with two dots below and three above it.

"Okay, focus your energy on it and open yourself to feel the communication," I said.

Dancing Moon exclaimed excitedly, "Oh yes, I can feel the connection being made."

The symbol started to glow, and a voice from somewhere within it said, "Acceptance. Do you wish to know about acceptance?"

"Yes, I do," Dancing Moon replied.

"When you are in the space of acceptance, you acknowledge that the present moment is whole and complete as it should be. Resisting what is means struggling against not just the moment itself, but against the entire universe. Instead of resistance, you have the choice to not fight. You decide to accept things and the universe as they are, rather than as you wish them to be."

Dancing Moon asked, "Is it wrong to wish for things to be different?"

"It is not wrong to desire a different future. You can always do that, but you must accept things as they are in the present moment. When you truly embrace acceptance, you understand deep within your heart that every problem carries an opportunity for spiritual growth. However, you must accept the moment as it is and extend your love to bring about transformation. By opening yourself to each situation and staying present in the moment, every moment of your life becomes as it should be.

"Always remember that just as you desire others to allow you to be who you are, you must also allow others to be who they are. When you truly accept others, their actions, behaviors, and beliefs will not trigger any negative energy, feelings, emotions, or thoughts within you. This grants you great freedom, as you become independent of any negative energies, feelings, emotions, and thoughts toward any person."

Dancing Moon questioned, "How can I be a teacher if I accept everything about everyone? Do I have to accept what is wrong with them?"

"When you accept others as they are, you can better help them because you do not perceive them as a problem. Your intention is to provide support, and your focus is not on judgment or blame. If you view any person as a problem, you will generate negative energy. However, if you utilize your will to offer support, you generate positive healing energy that allows them to be open to your teachings. By accepting others, you participate in the joy—not the pain—of any connection. Being in a state of acceptance enables you to always be focused on the spiritual essence of each situation involving any person," the symbol explained.

"Wow! That was incredible," Dancing Moon exclaimed.

"I told you that reading symbols would help you fulfill your purpose," I said.

"You did. I want to read another one. How about the one with two wavy lines?" Dancing Moon asked. She directed her energy toward the symbol, and soon it began to glow.

"You wish to know about the power of attention," a voice from within the symbol said.

"Yes," Dancing Moon affirmed.

"Whatever you direct your attention towards will grow stronger in your life. When you withdraw your attention, it will weaken and eventually disappear. The true force behind your attention is your intention, which triggers powerful transformational energy from the entire universe. This prompts the universe to send you opportunities, information, and physical manifestations that support the realization of your attention. The quality of your intention determines the amount of energy received from the universe, influencing the manifestation of what you desire in your life.

"The reason intention is so potent is that it embodies desire without attachment to the outcome. Desire alone is weak because desire is accompanied by negative 'must have' feelings that hinder your innate ability to create abundance. When your attention is focused on the present moment, you become more effective in manifesting your intended results. In present moment awareness, your intention is set on the future, but your attention remains in the present. This unleashes your power because the future is brought into existence in the present.

"The past, present, and future are all properties of consciousness. The past consists of recalled stored perceptions, the future is anticipation, and the present is awareness. Time is the movement of thought. Both the past and the future originate in the realm of imagination, whereas only the present, which is awareness, is real and eternal. The forces of creation are manifested in the present; they are not active in the past or the future. The genuine opportunity to take action based on the information sent to you by the universe exists solely in the present moment," the symbol conveyed.

"Thank you, Attention, for sharing your knowledge," Dancing Moon expressed her gratitude.

"Do you see the possibilities for learning and growth?" I asked. "These symbols can assist you in becoming a better teacher and guide."

"Oh yes, I see it clearly. This is a whole new way of learning, and it opens up a new world for me. I wonder which symbol relates to relationships. I must inquire about relationships because I believe my issues with time, obligation, and responsibility are connected to the importance I place on relationships."

"Why don't you try asking the wall? You might be surprised by what happens," I suggested.

"Okay, here I go." Dancing Moon turned back to face the wall. "Oh, powerful wall, tell me about the importance of relationships."

A symbol high on the wall began to glow, but I couldn't discern its markings or design. From within the symbol, a voice spoke, saying, "There is only one relationship that is truly important. It is the relationship that determines the quality of all the other relationships in your life. When that fundamental relationship is thriving, all other relationships in your life also flourish, and you experience harmony. Conversely, if that foundational relationship is not working, other relationships in your life will suffer, and you will feel out of balance.

"The one relationship that holds true importance is the relationship you have with your higher self, pure spiritual love. That is why, despite all your successes, you may still feel unfulfilled.

"You can utilize everyone and everything you encounter to deepen your connection with your higher self. By using your relationships to expand your relationship with your higher self, you can build more powerful and fulfilling connections with everyone and everything around you.

"When you neglect the improvement of your relationship with your higher self, you will feel that your life is not functioning optimally. Conflicts and fears may arise more frequently. While it may be easy to declare that you will focus on enhancing your relationship with your higher self, it can be challenging to resist the tendency of your mind to wander to other matters. There will be times when it is vital to withdraw completely from external relationships and concentrate on your relationship with your higher self. Eventually, you must re-engage with the world, using your connection with your higher self to relate to everything and everyone. This strengthens and empowers your commitment to living your life from a place of higher self and fulfilling your purpose.

"Directly focusing your energy on trying to mold the relationships around you in a particular way will not improve your life or your connections. However, you can use the relationships around you as vehicles for your spiritual growth. Your romantic relationship, in particular, possesses immense potential as a tool for spiritual development. The challenge lies in learning how to extract the lessons embedded in all your relationships to foster your spiritual growth. You must use your relationships as mirrors that reflect and facilitate your own inner process.

"After introspection, ask yourself if your inner processes allow you to perceive yourself as an artist whose life is their greatest masterpiece. This life is one where every moment is an opportunity for creation, brimming with infinite possibilities. Each moment presents a new chance, a new decision, and a new prospect to live your life imbued with unconditional love—to live from your higher self," the symbol conveyed its message.

"This is incredible!" Dancing Moon exclaimed. "I could engage in this forever. The knowledge and wisdom within this wall are astounding."

"Within your sanctuary, you have all the assistance you need. You can come here every day and open yourself to the divine flow of the universe," I assured her. Then, I paused and sniffed the air. "Do you smell that? Tobacco smoke?"

"Yes, I can smell it now. It's coming from Grandfather's room," Dancing Moon confirmed.

"He's calling us. You can explore more symbols later. Let's go and see him. I'll follow you."

We entered Grandfather's room and found the old man seated on the floor, smoking a red catlinite pipe. The presence of the pipe indicated his reverence for the Sioux nation, as they utilize catlinite in their ceremonial peace pipes. Then, Grandfather turned to Dancing Moon.

"Dancing Moon, you must assist society in learning our spiritual concepts. The sooner you begin teaching and guiding others back to the sacred path, the sooner our tribe, our nation and society will regain its health. I am deeply concerned for humanity."

"Our world is filled with a great deal of negative energy, emanating from the core of our human system. The world system doesn't honor the human heart, humanity, human relationships or Mother Earth. At the same time, the universe is moving toward higher love and higher spirituality. This may appear to be a duality, but it is not. The universe is just starting to ascend. As the universe's spiritual vibration rises, any system that does not support love, human relationships or spirituality will collapse."

"Every country has a strong system supporting fear; therefore, we live in a fear-based world human system. If our global society does not change its direction, it will collapse as the universe moves toward higher levels of spiritual awareness and love.

"You must not be overwhelmed by the negative picture I have painted. There's still an opportunity for the world to change its course. The burden is not yours alone. What I ask is that you do your part by being a spiritual teacher, healer and guide as the rest of the energies in your soul cluster are doing. That's enough to bring light into the planet and bring about the change that is required." Grandfather smiled warmly.

"I will do my best," Dancing Moon said. "I know now where to find help and support. If I feel overwhelmed, I will use my guides, and I will use you as well. I can hear your words within my heart now, as it is open. Thank you for asking Buffalo Feather to help me."

"You look exactly like Thunder Dog," I said to Grandfather.

"Yes, I know. He is here with me. He and I are always together. Where you see one, you also see the other. Our energy is the same. Now, come sit with me and smoke the sacred pipe as we honor White Buffalo Woman who brought us the sacred pipe. Let me tell both of you the story of how we received the sacred pipe.

"Two Sioux tribesmen were hunting and they saw something that looked like a rare and sacred white buffalo approaching from the distant horizon. As the figure drew close, they observed a beautiful woman, dressed in white buckskin. Her hair hung loose on the right, but the left side was tied with buffalo hair. She carried a bundle wrapped in a buffalo hide.

"She sang a sacred song as she walked slowly toward them. One of the men had evil thoughts about this maiden and moved toward her. The other hunter tried to restrain him, but the evil man pushed the good warrior away. A cloud descended on the evil one. When it lifted, his body was a skeleton being devoured by worms. This symbolized that the one who lives in ignorance and has evil in his heart may be destroyed by his own actions.

"The good hunter knelt in fear and trembled as the buckskin-clad woman approached. Gently she spoke to him and told him not to be afraid. She asked him to return to his people and prepare them for her coming. He did as she requested, and the beautiful woman appeared in their midst. While carrying the bowl of a pipe in her left hand and the stem in her right hand, she walked among them in a sun wise direction. She instructed the people regarding the use of the holy pipes.

'With this holy pipe you will walk through life filled with a living prayer,' she said. 'Your feet will rest upon Grandmother Earth. The stem will reach into the sky to the grandfather and your body will link the sacred earth beneath with the sacred sky above.'

"Wakan-Tanka smiles on us because now we are as one, Earth, Sky, all living things and human beings. Now we are one big family. The pipe binds us all together. As the woman walked away into the distance, she turned into a White Buffalo and disappeared on the horizon.

"Dancing Moon, you must remember the message of White Buffalo Woman. And always keep your heart filled with love. Let the Divine Creator's wisdom free your mind from ignorance and your loving actions will keep you on the path of divine light."

Dancing Moon took a draw of the sacred pipe. Then she said, "Mitakuye oyasin."

My mind filled with thoughts of Thunder Dog and White Buffalo Woman. Grandfather reminded me of how much I missed Thunder Dog and the time we shared together. This saddened my heart and a tear dropped onto my hand.

I looked at Grandfather and took a long, slow draw on the sacred pipe. Then I said, "Mitakuye oyasin."

"Dancing Moon, I am proud of the path you are taking," Grandfather said. "Now, go with my blessing. Your destiny awaits you. Buffalo Feather, Thunder Dog and I thank you. We are proud of the medicine man you have become. You are on the pathway. Go now. There are others who need your help."

Dancing Moon and I left Grandfather. I said good-bye to Grandmother and Feather as we walked back to the room with the rock.

"Dancing Moon, the battle between darkness and light continues," I stated. "Your powers as a teacher, healer, and guide are needed. If you persist in prayer, meditation, and visiting your sacred sanctuary, your path will become easier. Simply continue removing the barriers that obstruct the flow of your spiritual love, and your way will become clear."

As our tears streamed down our faces, we embraced each other.

"I will remember and practice all that I have learned," she assured me. "I will call upon you and my guides for support. My purpose is clear, and the Divine Creator illuminates my pathway. I will follow his teachings and live my life in love and unity with all. Thank you, Buffalo Feather. I think I'll remain here a little longer; I'm not quite ready to leave yet."

"Goodbye, Dancing Moon. Goodbye, Rock," I bid them farewell.

It was a bright and beautiful day. I strolled through the vibrant poppy field, relishing the sights and scents, when a monarch butterfly landed on my head. Instantly, I found myself back in the sweat lodge.

"Welcome back, Buffalo Feather. We have been awaiting your return. The first endurance has been completed," Naomi greeted me.

"Mitakuye oyasin," I whispered softly.

Crying Wolf opened the flap, allowing the cool outside air to rush in and embrace the lodge. It felt refreshing as it circulated around my body and throughout the sacred space.

"Buffalo Feather, as you just experienced, there are many ways to teach, heal, and guide others back to the spiritual light," Naomi explained. "Sharing your wisdom on the astral plane is an effective means of aiding those around you. Each of us possesses a soul and several bodies or planes. Our visible body functions on the physical plane, serving as the vessel through which we engage with the lower world. We also possess other bodies that are imperceptible to ordinary sight. These bodies enable us to navigate the emotional, mental, and spiritual realms."

"Encountering Dancing Moon on the astral plane was an extraordinary experience," I remarked. "I am grateful to Thunder Dog for teaching me about my astral body and how to utilize all the planes for spiritual work. Thanks to him, I understand that each of our bodies provides a unique way to communicate and gain profound insights into our true nature."

"I witnessed your ego mind's dissolution, leading to a transformation of your consciousness. Could you feel the ease with which divine energy flowed to you once your ego was no longer present?" Naomi inquired.

"Yes, I did. It was a remarkable and healing experience," I replied.

Chapter 11

SKELETON SPIRIT

Naomi signaled for her helpers to close the flap, enveloping us in darkness. After a few moments, the helpers passed in seven stones, one by one, before swiftly closing the flap again. The red-orange glow emanating from the stones held a hypnotic sway over me. A peculiar sensation coursed through my entire body as Naomi sprinkled four cups of water and some sweet grass onto the scorching stones. Dizziness washed over me, and the entire lodge seemed to transform into a vibrant shade of red. Amidst the gradual spinning of the room, Naomi commenced singing a sacred song, paying homage to the four directions.

Suddenly, something swiftly flew past my head, too fast for me to discern its nature. Moments later, it darted by in the opposite direction, affording me a better glimpse. It appeared to be a diminutive human skeleton, encircled by a greenish light. The face seemed to exhibit a fusion of human and animal features, with teeth resembling those of a mountain lion or some other feline creature—long, sharp, and menacing.

Shortly after, another greenish light whizzed past me, disappearing as quickly as it had appeared. After a few minutes, the light returned and hovered right before my eyes, studying me intently.

In the background, Naomi's voice resonated, "Oh, great Divine Creator, I call upon the spirits who have transcended this earthly plane. We seek their energy and insights to facilitate our transition to the next level of spiritual awareness."

Soon after, the greenish skeleton vanished, leaving behind a lingering intensity. An unsettling unease and tension gripped me. My heart raced, and my breathing quickened. Suddenly, a loud crack reverberated from a distance, accompanied by a blinding flash of light. I began to turn my head to glance at Black Hawk, but five miniature skeletons materialized, hovering about six inches from my face, seemingly appearing out of thin air. All of them displayed their long, menacing teeth.

Naomi's words echoed in my mind, "There will be many potent energies entering the lodge. You may feel frightened, but try to endure. If you find the presence of these spirits too overwhelming, please call out, and I will temporarily halt the ceremony so that you may exit through the doorway."

As I delved into meditation, summoning the spiritual light within me, one of the skeletons lunged at my neck and bit down on a tobacco prayer tie. Its teeth sank into the tie, ripping and tugging at the tobacco within. The sensation of its sharp teeth pressing against my skin filled me with fear. Just then, a small warrior carrying an illuminated lance entered the lodge, directing his white light towards the crown of my head. Through the warrior's presence, a clear insight flooded my consciousness as he infused the lodge with healing energy.

The warrior spoke, "I am here to provide guidance regarding the fear skeleton. Fear is the absence of love. Its essence stems from this absence, which renders it impervious to direct action. Fear energy is akin to darkness—it cannot be manipulated or discarded. There is only one way to relate to darkness: by turning on the light. Similarly, to rid your life of fear, you must embrace your spiritual light. By understanding the nature of darkness, you gain insight into the true nature of fear.

Buffalo Feather, you are spirit, and thus possess an eternal light capable of dispelling fear from your life.

"Love is the light, and fear is the darkness. If you fixate on fear, you will forever remain entangled within its grasp, as you attempt to contend with darkness directly. However, this is an impossibility since darkness does not truly exist. If you engage in a protracted struggle against darkness, you will find yourself lost in a futile battle, trapped within a state of unconsciousness. Your efforts will ultimately deplete you, draining your life force and diminishing your awareness. Fear prevents you from living from your higher self.

"Buffalo Feather, when fear consumes you, recognize that your ego mind has ensnared you within an unnatural state. By accepting a situation that has already transpired, you reconnect with your spiritual energy, and it flows within you. This spiritual flow activates your divine light, dispelling the darkness. Fear dissolves into nonexistence.

As I focused my spiritual light on the fear skeleton, it vanished, taking a portion of the tobacco with it. However, another skeleton promptly appeared and clamped its teeth onto the same tie.

The warrior continued, "Now, I shall address Anger. Many people believe that some anger is justified, but this belief does not align with Divine truth. This does not imply that you should berate yourself for experiencing anger or suppress its expression. Repressed anger accumulates and becomes ingrained within your being.

"If anger becomes your default state, you will perpetually reside in a realm of internal rage. You will find yourself waiting for something or someone to provoke you, and when that provocation arises, you temporarily descend into madness. This madness lies beyond your control, causing you to fluctuate in and out of anger continuously.

"There is no need to direct your anger towards anyone. You can release anger through prayer, meditation, taking a long walk, or going for a run. There are numerous ways to let go of anger without lashing out at someone or something. To transcend anger, you must not only focus on releasing negative energy but also shift your attention towards love. Let your loving light dispel the darkness of anger."

As I immersed myself in meditation, the skeleton disappeared, taking some of the tobacco with it. Another skeleton promptly bit into the tie, and a sense of guilt washed over me.

The warrior explained, "This is the skeleton of guilt. All feelings of guilt reside within your ego mind and hold no spiritual essence. Not everything is within your control. You possess the power to determine how you interpret past events. While a situation may appear as though it could have unfolded differently, perhaps it could not have. The divine plan unfolds, and we follow the path laid out for us. What happens to us is not the defining element of our human experience; it is how we navigate and respond to the situation that shapes the quality of our experience. Enlightenment occurs when we remember our spiritual nature, regardless of the event or circumstance."

All guilt resides in a non-existent past. All you can do is accept what exists in the present and exercise your free will.

"By adopting a spiritual perspective, your past dissolves, and you live in the present moment. Your spirituality does not exist within the confines of time; it is eternal and ever-present. You can only know the Divine Creator by looking inward and forward. If you dwell in the past and live in yesterday, you will never encounter the Divine Creator.

"You cannot attain a guilt-free existence by fixating on events that have occurred in time. Liberation from guilt is only achieved by transcending time. Your spiritual consciousness exists beyond the constraints of time. If you remain aware, you will know the truth. Stay awake and let your light flow."

I began singing a sacred song, and the fragrance of apple sage filled the air. The Guilt skeleton took some of the tobacco and departed. Naomi and Black Hawk joined me in the song.

When another skeleton bit into the same tie as the previous ones, the warrior addressed it, saying, "This is the skeleton of worry. When you worry, you squander your energy because you fail to utilize your power to establish an eternal connection with the Divine Creator.

"You must cease worrying and embrace life with the understanding that you are eternal and loved by the Divine Creator. Your spirit is love and will never perish. It is your ego mind that fabricates the illusion of something or someone to worry about. No one is against you, and you are not in competition with anyone. There is only one spirit and one being present. Do not succumb to the illusion of separation, believing there are many separate individuals. Everyone is a manifestation of the Divine Creator, and everything is interconnected."

As I continued to sing, the skeleton of worry vanished. However, another skeleton bit into the tie, engulfing me in sorrow.

The warrior conveyed, "Sorrow is a creation of the ego mind. The physical world is in constant flux, and life is perpetually beautiful. There is nothing wrong. Since there is no yesterday or tomorrow, there is nothing to cause sorrow.

"If you experience sadness, it is because you are clinging to the past. You are dwelling on what was or what could have been, clinging to that which no longer exists. Your true essence is eternal and ever-present. The longing to remain in a state of sadness emerges from a mind that perceives itself as separate from the whole, a mind that believes it has lost something irreplaceable. It believes that the past is gone. However, this deep yearning deprives you of fully experiencing the present moment, which is here and now. The present is the only true moment of existence, and with spiritual awareness, each moment becomes eternal."

All five skeletons reappeared and bit into the same prayer tie, pulling at it until it started to come loose. Suddenly, the tie, the skeletons, and the warrior vanished, leaving behind the scent of fresh basil. My breathing became slower and more even, and a profound sense of inner peace washed over me. The basil had a soothing effect.

"The second endurance is complete," Naomi announced.

"Mitakuye oyasin," I whispered softly.

Crying Wolf opened the flap, allowing the air to rush inside, cooling the lodge.

Chapter 12

CARDOVA

I was fast asleep when the warning bell went off in my mind. I moved slowly from the threshold of real sleep towards clarity and wakefulness. As I approached the awakened state my sense of alarm grew. Something was wrong. I felt a physical presence in the room. I opened my eyes, and looked to my left. Nothing was out of place. I sat up and looked right, everything was as it should be, but still I sensed something or someone nearby.

There was a strong smell of jasmine, honeysuckle and sweet attar in the air. These fragrances caused me to think of Thunder Dog.

The clock showed two a.m.

"My god it's early." I thought.

The feeling of being watched didn't leave. I carefully inventoried every inch of the room, but nothing was out of place. After a few minutes of searching and sensing in vain I lay back in bed, closed my eyes, and tried to relax.

In just a few moments the feeling of uneasiness returned. This time however I felt as though I were being watched by a thousand eyes. In a state of nervous incoherence, I sprang out of bed and looked around. I didn't see anything unusual, but I felt a cool breeze coming from a window that wasn't open. Goose bumps rose on my arms.

"Someone is in here." I thought.

"Who's there?" I asked.

There was no answer.

"Thunder Dog is that you?" I asked.

Still no answer.

That feeling of being watched persisted. I felt the strong energy of another.

"I can feel it so why can't I see it?" I thought.

In my mind, Thunder Dog voiced answered. "Because your five senses work on such a basic conditioned response level it is quite easy to hide from them. You don't see what is there; you see what you are looking for. In fact, you see what is stored in the great memory bank in your mind. To perceive that which does not want to be seen you must use your senses differently. You must open your awareness to other realities and use your spiritual intention to enhance your sensory capability to support you in seeing that which desires to remain concealed. Then and only then will the unseen be revealed."

Automatically and instantaneously, I knew what to do.

I closed my eyes and focused my consciousness on the fear that had started to build within me. After a few moments some of the anxiety slipped away. As I became more relaxed and focused, my awareness of an alien presence grew. When completely relaxed I opened my eyes and tilted my head to the right. I didn't try to focus on anything in particular, but instead on everything around me.

I thought, "this is just like meditating, when I allow everything to come into my awareness without focusing on any one thing."

I thought I saw an image. Something was there. The image was a little hazy and it shimmered like a mirage. I tilted my head a little more and saw a tall Native American man with shoulder-length white hair, sitting at the foot of my bed. After my initial shock, I began to carefully study him. He was dressed in a black silk oriental robe. In one hand he held a wooden walking stick with an eagle feather fastened near the top, in the other he had a deer skin rattle. His smooth, creamy complexion made it difficult to judge his age; he could have been anywhere between thirty and fifty years old.

"He looks like a man, but he or it isn't a man. The energy is wrong, way wrong, and this wrong energy is filling the room. In fact, this wrongness is growing and expanding minute by minute. This man thing is at the center of this energy." I thought.

It had been hard to see him because he was bending the moon light from the window all around him so that he was concealed in a cocoon of transparent energy.

He realized at once that I could see him.

"So, you're the great Buffalo Feather, the substitute Medicine Man," he said with contempt.

"Who are you? What are you?" I asked.

"I am not a 'who,' but... perhaps I am a 'what'," he replied, followed by a sardonic laugh.

"What do you want?" I asked, my voice tinged with caution.

"I have what I want. I am not a mere 'man thing.' I am a master sorcerer, unmatched on this earth. So, instead of thinking of me as a 'man thing,' 'sorcerer' will suffice until I deem it necessary to reveal my name," he stated with an air of arrogance.

He can read my thoughts, I realized.

Mentally, I heard Thunder Dog's voice saying, "Things are not always as they seem. Reality, as you perceive it, is far less substantial than your mind would like to believe. By allowing your spirit to guide you, your actions can transcend the need for prior thought. To achieve this state of spiritual awareness, reconnect your physical self with the divine creator. Only then will your choices be genuine."

"I will refer to you as Sorcerer," I declared.

"Are you still seeking Thunder Dog's guidance? I am quite surprised, and yes, more than a little disappointed in you. After three years of studying with Thunder Dog and Naomi, the great Buffalo Feather is still following a voice in his head called Thunder Dog. Perhaps Thunder Dog existed long ago and may have been a formidable Medicine Man, but his time has passed. Surely, you must know that by now," the sorcerer sneered.

I could feel the malignant energy emanating from the sorcerer pressing against my body, forcing me to recline. The fragrant scent of flowers had been replaced by the stench of stagnant water.

"What do you know of Thunder Dog?" I defiantly inquired.

After a prolonged pause, the Sorcerer replied, "Thunder Dog was one of my most promising students, Grasshopper. 'Grasshopper'... that is one of your words," the sorcerer smirked contemptuously.

"What do you want?" I asked again, determined to understand his intentions.

"When I first arrived here, my plan was to invite you to join me. However, having witnessed your abilities, or rather, your lack thereof, I am beginning to question if it is worth my time. I thought you were ready to learn the art of crossing, but now I see that Thunder Dog and Naomi did a poor job in your training. You are not prepared. You remain oblivious, trapped within the confines of this physical world. You still rely too heavily on language and rationality. You were not even aware of my presence until I desired for you to know. I had to create a breeze as a clue," the sorcerer lamented.

"If I am not what you seek, then leave," I said, a glimmer of hope in my voice.

"Perhaps I will. But you still do not know who I am. Did Thunder Dog inform you that I would come to train you?" the sorcerer queried.

"I need time to think," I thought to myself, desperately wanting him and his malevolent energy to depart.

"If I am not ready, it does not matter whether Thunder Dog informed me of your arrival or not," I asserted.

"What are you trying to accomplish? Provoke me?" I silently pondered.

His energy intensified, pressing against my body with even greater force, causing significant discomfort.

"You won't be rid of me so easily," the sorcerer declared.

His energy field transitioned from discomfort to pain as he concentrated his force on my chest. The pressure felt as though someone was standing on my chest with both feet, while the sorcerer smirked.

"I must do something," I thought urgently.

Closing my eyes, I turned my focus inward to the core of my being. From there, I directed my intention outward, aiming to confront his energy field. Opening my eyes, I met his gaze directly. His green eyes, filled with the depth that comes from years of meditation, met mine. They were fiery yet tranquil. Locking my gaze onto his, I summoned all my willpower to push back against his force field. After a few moments, I felt the pressure from his energy ease slightly.

"It's working," I thought, a glimmer of hope rekindled within me.

In the distance, I heard the melodic sound of wind chimes resonating from outside my window.

"They sound like ceremonial temple bells," I reflected, intrigued by their ethereal tones.

My concentration was abruptly shattered, and the energy field struck my chest with even greater force, causing me to cry out in pain involuntarily.

"Oh, Buffalo Feather, you were making progress. However, you must learn to discipline your mind. It was a valiant attempt, but even if you had maintained your intent, I doubt I would have dropped the energy field," the sorcerer taunted sarcastically.

Without uttering a word, I refocused my intention on his energy field, determined to persist.

"I have observed you closely over the past few years, and what impresses me about you is your persistence. You may not possess great power in the realm of sorcery, but your desire is stronger than most, and your will is not easily broken. Yes, I must admit that your relentlessness and unwavering pursuit are among your strongest qualities. I shall call you Buffalo Relentless Feather," the sorcerer chuckled.

Continuing to maintain my focus on the sorcerer's energy field, I suddenly realized that it had vanished. Sitting up in bed, I took a deep breath, relishing the sensation of fresh air filling my lungs. I could move freely once again, relieved to see the energy field gone.

"Why did you remove the energy field? And no, I'm not sorry to see it disappear," I inquired.

"You could simply say 'thanks.' I cannot remain here indefinitely, waiting for you to realize that my will and energy surpasses yours. Besides, the sun is rising, and it is time for me to cross over to explore other worlds," the sorcerer replied smugly.

"You keep speaking of crossing over and other worlds. What do you mean?" I questioned; my curiosity piqued.

"Why did I ask that? I don't really want to know about other worlds; I simply want him to leave," I thought to myself.

"Perhaps Thunder Dog taught you more than I anticipated. Maybe you are employing some of your opossum energy against me. I sensed a strong opossum presence when I entered your reality. Wouldn't you dare attempt to deceive Cardova?" the sorcerer questioned.

In that moment, the sorcerer realized his slip of revealing something about himself prematurely.

"Who is Cardova? Is that your name?" I inquired with a mischievous smile.

"Yes, Cardova is my name. You possess the strong energies of opossum and fox. We must have a conversation, but not here, not in this bounded reality of time," Cardova confirmed.

Directly behind the sorcerer, a dark passageway materialized, the size of an ordinary door. Though darkness enveloped its interior, the sound of ocean waves emanated from within.

Instantly, fear gripped me, and I felt a surge of panic.

"Fear not. If I intended to harm you, I would have done so already. That little energy field was merely a test. If you choose to accompany me, I will answer all your questions and more. You will discover much about yourself and Thunder Dog. I will reveal the past, present, pleasure, and future to you," Cardova offered.

I felt his energy field return, but this time, I was fully enfolded within it.

"I am like a neatly packaged parcel, ready for shipment. Though I have no idea where I am being sent. Can he forcibly transport me to another world if I resist him with my own energy?" I wondered.

"Yes, I possess the power to coerce you to come with me, but I will not. Buffalo Feather, allow your intuition to guide you to the realization that moving between worlds was part of Thunder Dog's training. Shifting between realities is the 'crossing' I spoke of. Simply relax and experience the crossing for yourself. You have crossed over numerous times before. Remember when you entered the Owl and soared with him? Or when you encountered Dancing Moon in her sanctuary? Both instances were forms of crossing over. However, you did not cross as a sorcerer because your intent was askew. Only when your positive and negative forces are perfectly aligned will you sense or perceive the opening in the energy surrounding you that leads to other worlds. Without this balance, crossing over unassisted is impossible," Cardova explained.

"For how long have you been observing me? Spying on me? Tracking me?" I demanded.

"There will be ample time for questions. Are you coming with me or not? Stop stalling. I will not fall for your opossum trickery again. Buffalo Feather, trust your spirit and release your calculating mind. Do not let your suspicious nature dictate that I depart," Cardova insisted.

"Why should I accompany you?" I asked, maintaining my suspicion.

"Don't you want to know how I've managed to keep track of you all this time? Don't you think it's time to continue your training?" Cardova inquired.

"Neither Thunder Dog nor Naomi ever mentioned you or your role in my training. Furthermore, your energy feels entirely different from what I've encountered before," I stated.

"But do you know why my energy feels off to you?" Cardova countered cleverly.

"Why?" I inquired.

"Join me, and I will provide answers to all your questions. However, I will reveal this much now: one reason my energy feels different is that I am pure spirit. I am not a spiritual being inhabiting a human body like you and Thunder Dog were," Cardova explained.

"Why should I trust you? How can I be certain that you're not attempting to deceive me by fabricating this entire situation? Thunder Dog never mentioned anything about you," I questioned.

"Of course, I am lying. You seem to forget that you reside in a world of deception. Remember that you have chosen to exist within a realm of time, space, and perception. In your world, the closest approximation to truth is merely an illusion. But nothing can truly be the truth, for as a human being, your perception is inherently limited. To transcend this illusion, you must step outside the false narrative of who you believe yourself to be. Perception creates a distorted and constrained picture of reality. Rest assured, the words you perceive from me are lies. In fact, one reason for you to accompany me to a world I have constructed is to escape this limited reality of yours," Cardova laughed.

"You certainly have a way with words," I remarked.

"You simply dislike it when I speak the words you should be uttering. Come with me. If you do, you will discover that I have known you since you were eight years old," Cardova revealed.

My fear fluctuated like a roller coaster, and my mind raced uncontrollably.

"I need to calm down," I reminded myself. "There is nothing to fear but fear itself. If Cardova intended to harm me, he would have done so already. Besides, there is something strangely familiar about him. Has he truly known me since I was eight? And what does he mean by being pure spirit?" I pondered.

Thunder Dog's voice resonated within me. "To attain higher levels of awareness, you must master your inner emotions. Fear is one of the most formidable emotions you must overcome on your earthly journey. To assist you in confronting fear, the Divine Creator has bestowed upon you the power of free choice. However, to harness the true power of free choice, you must possess unwavering spiritual faith and operate from a higher consciousness. Trust, Buffalo Feather, trust," Thunder Dog's words echoed.

I contemplated Thunder Dog's profound wisdom. "He has a way of getting to the heart of the matter. Perhaps it is indeed time for my training to continue," I concluded.

"Thank you, Thunder Dog," I expressed my gratitude aloud.

"Very well, I will accompany you," I declared, my curiosity and excitement now reaching their peak.

"Excellent. It won't cause you any harm. Let your training commence, Grasshopper," Cardova smiled.

Cardova vanished into the dark passageway that had materialized behind him. The energy field tightly enveloped my body, and I felt myself being drawn towards the passageway. Fear still lingered within me, but I made the decision not to resist. Holding my breath, I entered the darkness.

From deeper within the passageway, the sound of waves crashing against the shore reached my ears. I caught a whiff of the fresh ocean breeze.

In the midst of the darkness, a small butterfly emitted its own radiant light. The butterfly approached me and halted about two feet away from my face. After hovering for a moment, the luminous insect changed direction and proceeded further into the obscurity. Automatically, my intention fixated on it, and I followed closely behind. I noticed that I was no longer encompassed by Cardova's energy field. The moment the butterfly appeared; the wrapping disappeared. Although the butterfly's glow didn't illuminate the passageway, it seemed to be in communication with me. Our intentions were intertwined, and it led the way through the corridor, utilizing the force of its intention. Since my intention was linked with the butterfly's, my movements matched its flight path.

As I navigated through the darkness, a bright light appeared, transforming the passageway into a tunnel with an opening at the far end. Once I emerged from the tunnel, I found myself suspended in the light. Taking in my surroundings, I discovered a scene reminiscent of early medieval times. A thermal spring flowed out from the side of a cliff, pouring into a steaming pool. I somehow knew the temperature of the thermal water to be around 110 degrees. Nearby, a brown bear feasted on a sockeye salmon plucked from a nearby stream.

I realized I stood atop a high grassy bluff overlooking an ocean with a long white sandy beach. Abundant lush plants and towering green palm trees surrounded the area.

"But which ocean is this? Into what world or time period have I crossed?" unease filled my thoughts.

For the first time, I became aware of my nudity. I had been abruptly taken from my bed at 2 a.m., left in the raw on this hot night.

Before I could fully process the situation, I felt myself descending and landed with a thud, sprawling clumsily on the ground.

"You didn't just cross over; you leaped over. If you keep crash-landing like that, you'll break your ass. Nice pose, though. Perhaps the first thing I should teach you is how to land without bumping your rear. If birds can do it without bumping their butts, so can you," Cardova laughed.

I looked at Cardova, who sported a smile on his face.

"Let's have a conversation over there," Cardova pointed toward a cave roughly 100 yards away.

I followed Cardova to the cave, peering inside its small and dark entrance.

"After you," Cardova gestured for me to enter.

I stepped into the dimly lit cave, where the chamber was so tight that my shoulders brushed against the cold walls. I turned around and settled on the ground, leaning my back against the rough, jagged rocks, with my legs crossed.

"Why would he choose to talk in this cave when there's ample open space outside?" I wondered.

Cardova entered the cave, and I noticed that the chamber walls expanded to accommodate him. The portion of the cave Cardova occupied seemed much more spacious than mine. The rocks around him appeared smooth and comfortable, while the chamber walls behind him emitted a soft backlight.

As I observed, the rock walls and ceiling behind Cardova started losing their color and solidity. Within a few seconds, the cave ceased to exist, revealing a breathtaking ocean and a pristine sandy beach below.

"Why does Cardova have more space and light than I do? Is this cave alive?" my thoughts raced.

Cardova settled on the ground, crossing his legs. A fire pit materialized halfway between us. Cardova waved his hands in circular motions above the pit, igniting a fire.

The warmth of the red flames felt soothing against my legs, easing my tension. "Let me try to focus on why I'm here," I thought.

"Are you ready to answer my questions?" I asked eagerly, starting to feel somewhat at ease in this peculiar situation.

"Yes, I will tell you about the past, present, pleasure, and the future," Cardova replied.

"Alright, my first question about the past is: What do you mean when you say you have known me since I was eight years old?" I inquired.

"I mean exactly what I said. We first crossed paths when you were eight years old. In fact, one could say that I saved your life," Cardova smiled.

"I don't understand. I have clear memories of my childhood, and I don't remember you. Truly, I have no recollection of you. Are all your answers going to be riddles?" I asked, seeking clarification.

"You can't remember me because I existed in a different form. But let's see if I can help you make sense of it all," Cardova assured me.

Cardova retrieved a small pouch made of three types of animal skin from his robe. Opening the bag, he withdrew what appeared to be a handful of white powder and sprinkled it into the fire. Instantly, green flames leaped high in the air, casting eerie shadows on the walls.

"Oh, great spirits, help my brother remember a time, space, and place where he battled the evil spider spirit," Cardova invoked, repeating the words "Buffalo Feather, remember... remember... remember" in a meditative chant.

A wispy green smoke rose from the fire pit, gradually drifting toward me. Instinctively, I tried to move backward, but the rock wall behind me prevented any retreat. I glanced at Cardova, who had closed his eyes and continued his rhythmic chanting.

The smoke inched closer until it hovered in front of my third eye. Then, it entered my forehead, causing an immediate burst of vibrant colors and a tingling sensation in my lower body. I felt myself rapidly remembering events from the past, witnessing a multitude of experiences, yet comprehending very little due to the overwhelming speed. Eventually, the backward journey halted, and I found myself back in the house where I grew up.

I observed myself lying in bed, asleep as an eight-year-old. As my awareness merged with that younger version of myself, I kept my consciousness just beyond his grasp. Although I could sense the boy's mind, I was certain he remained unaware of my presence.

Knowing it was crucial to remain in the background and allow the experience to unfold as it had years ago, I found it easier to let it play out, reassured by the knowledge that I had survived.

The sound of my mother entering the room stirred me from a light sleep. She woke my brothers, and as she left the room, I greeted her with a cheerful "Good morning, Mom." She nodded in acknowledgment. Glancing at the clock on the wall, I saw it was 5:00 a.m. Time to rise and catch the bus to DiGeorge's vineyard for a day of grape cutting.

My brothers and I got up swiftly, dressing in silence. Once ready, we left the house and embarked on the short walk to the bus stop. The cold morning air enveloped us as we walked along Brighten Road, eventually reaching Cottonwood Road, where the old blue and green bus patiently awaited anyone seeking work. Boarding the bus, we proceeded to the back and took our seats.

As we passed by, someone greeted us with a friendly "Hi, Hooks." Each of my brothers responded with a "hello," but I remained silent, continuing my stride. Settling by the window, I closed my eyes, hoping to catch an extra hour of sleep before reaching the vineyard. The drowsiness overcame me, and soon I drifted back into slumber.

The jolting of the bus pulling out of the parking lot to head for the vineyard stirred me awake, albeit not enough to keep me from dozing off once more. I found myself awakening again when the bus came to a halt, and I peered out the window. We had arrived at DiGeorge's vineyard, surrounded by luscious grapes. One by one, people disembarked from the bus, invigorated by the morning air. It was approximately 7:30 a.m., and everyone seemed eager to commence cutting grapes. However, I felt no enthusiasm to leave the bus or start working. All I desired was to stay there and sleep for another hour or two.

Eventually, everyone had left the bus, except my brothers and me. We exchanged glances for a few moments until Charles spoke up, saying, "Come on, girls, let's get to work. The sooner we start, the sooner we finish." He swiftly rose and walked off, singing a lively tune. My brothers followed suit, joining in the song. Finally, I reluctantly rose from my seat, head down, and made my way off the bus.

Jimmie turned to me, sensing something amiss. "What's wrong? You don't seem like yourself this morning," he remarked softly.

"I don't know. I have a strange feeling about today, but maybe it'll pass," I replied in a hushed tone.

Together, my brothers and I entered the vineyard, selecting our respective rows of grapes to cut. The process was simple yet effective. We positioned a few plastic buckets along the row every 5 to 10 feet and positioned ourselves beneath a grapevine. Armed with buckets and a sharp knife with a curved blade specifically designed for cutting grapes, we examined the bunches, carefully selecting only the sun-ripened ones and placing them in our buckets. Once a bucket was full, we retrieved another and continued the process.

After filling six to ten buckets, we would carry them two at a time to the end of our rows, where a large metal bin awaited along with the inspector. Dumping the grapes into the bin, the inspector closely examined their quality and the fullness of our buckets. If everything met the inspector's standards, he or she would mark the approved buckets in our total account. However, if the quality was deemed unsatisfactory, the inspector wouldn't give us credit for those grapes.

Failure to address the issues pointed out by the inspector would prompt a call to the foreman. Failure to address the issues pointed out by the inspector would prompt a call to the foreman. The foreman would assist us, and he had the authority to terminate our employment. However, there were always plenty of people available to teach the art of cutting grapes if we were willing to correct any problems.

At the end of the day, we would be paid based on the number of buckets recorded in the inspector's record book. My brothers and I always had the inspector add each bucket to the Hooks' account. Whenever one of us approached the inspector, he would say, "Add these to the Hooks' account."

As the intense yellow sun ascended in the east, it quickly warmed the moist air, signaling the start of our day's work. Soon, my brothers and I found ourselves beneath the vines, cutting grapes with the precision of a well-oiled machine. Hour after hour passed as we tirelessly cut and carried buckets of grapes to the end of the row for inspection.

Several hours crept by, and the sun reached its zenith, transforming into a blazing red orb that intensified the scorching heat of the day. It was during this time, after dropping off two buckets, that I felt a sting on the back of my neck. Instinctively, I swatted at it, assuming it was a bee or some other insect. Returning to my position under the vine, I resumed cutting grapes, though I noticed I was sweating more profusely than usual, even for such a hot day. Nevertheless, I persisted for another hour.

As I made my way to the end of the row, carrying two buckets, the world around me suddenly began to spin. It spun faster and faster, causing me to collapse to the ground. My mind drifted in and out of a dreamlike state as vivid images materialized from the shadows. Fear would be replaced by laughter and joy in a matter of moments.

Brilliant colors swirled through my mind as a sharp, crisp sound echoed in the distance. I felt myself caught in a labyrinth of exotic sights, sounds, colors, motion, and emotions. Suddenly, I found myself soaring high in the sky, riding on the back of a gigantic hawk. Looking down, I witnessed a vast Native American tribe and an immense herd of buffalo stretching over the mountains as far as the eye could see. The sight of the beautiful buffalo captivated me.

Drifting in and out of consciousness, I floated between the realm of reality and a realm of illusions. At times, I would briefly return to solid reality, only to be whisked away again to a world beyond imagination. Dragons, colossal butterflies, lions, tigers, and all sorts of fantastical creatures surrounded me, appearing real and close enough to touch. I leapt onto the back of a mighty lion and rode across a field of purple lilies, followed by exhilarating adventures atop larger animals.

Some of the creatures gave chase, sparking both fear and excitement within me. Yet, I couldn't help but feel joyous and laugh amidst the thrilling encounters.

Suddenly, I found myself in the midst of a baseball game, standing on the pitcher's mound adorned with the number 42. It was the bottom of the ninth inning, with my team leading by one run. The bases were loaded, and there were two outs. The coach emerged from the dugout and approached me.

"We only need one more out to win the game and become the league champions for the first time ever. Can you continue? You've pitched an incredible game so far, but I want to bring in a relief pitcher to finish it off," the coach said.

"No, Coach, please. I can finish the game," I replied, determined to see it through.

"All you have to do is get this last batter out, and we win. He's their best home run hitter. He excels under pressure and in critical situations," the coach explained.

"I can do it," I affirmed.

"Do you see who you're pitching to?" the coach asked.

For the first time, I glanced at the batter standing in the box. To my astonishment, it was none other than myself. I was pitching to my own reflection.

"I'm pitching to myself. How is that possible?" I questioned.

"That's right—you're pitching to yourself. You have only one conflict to resolve in order to win the game, and that conflict lies within you. That's also the ultimate solution for winning the game of life. Remember, as you make your next pitch, use the clarity that arises from conflict to guide the baseball. Don't be afraid of yourself," the coach advised before briskly returning to the dugout.

Stepping back onto the pitcher's mound, I focused my gaze on the batter. The catcher signaled for a fastball, and I acknowledged his call. Beginning my windup, I hurled the baseball with all my might, feeling a satisfying release as it left my right hand. My follow-through was flawless as the ball gained velocity. My consciousness shifted to being in the batter's box, readying myself to swing at the swiftly approaching ball. The ball neared the batter's box, and a few drops of sweat formed on my forehead as I unleashed a powerful swing.

Suddenly, I jolted awake from my dreamy state, finding myself in my bed at home. My brother Roy sat by my bedside, and as my eyes closed again, I slipped back into a dream world. This time, I engaged in a conversation with an ancient African medicine man.

"Fear not, for I am here to assist you. You must not succumb to your fears. Join me, and together we can combat the evil spirits that assail you. Our combined power can vanquish the negative demons seeking to strip you of your strength," the medicine man conveyed. Drifting off once more, I left the African medicine man behind.

When I regained consciousness again, I discovered myself in my bed, the sheets drenched in sweat. Mom, Dad, and my brothers gathered around me, drawing closer in a huddle.

"Where am I? What happened?" I inquired.

"You were bitten by a spider while working in the vineyard. The doctor believes it might have been a black widow or another venomous spider," Mom explained.

"You collapsed on your way back after dropping off a bucket of grapes," Charles added.

Mom continued, "You've been unconscious and incoherent for the past five days. The doctor was uncertain about the treatment since he wasn't certain about the type of spider bite. The antidote didn't yield a positive response from you. He was at a loss, and your fever continued to rise. That's when I reached out to the African medicine man. I implored him to help you."

The group of individuals she referred to were a small community of Africans who clung to their traditional ways as best they could. They kept to themselves and practiced various forms of magic and African medicine. The townsfolk often joked about their black magic and voodoo dolls, but we were unaware of their medical practices. Mom must have been desperate to seek their aid.

"I went to the African village and explained the situation to the first person I encountered. They directed me to the medicine man, and I relayed everything to him," Mom shared, tears welling up in her eyes.

"I must see him immediately. We cannot afford to waste any time," the medicine man insisted.

"Yes, let's hurry!" Mom responded.

We rushed to our old station wagon and drove swiftly toward home. It felt as though the medicine man had anticipated my arrival long before I reached his village.

"Once inside our house, the medicine man surveyed the surroundings meticulously before attending to you. He entered your bedroom and began unpacking items from his medicine bag, placing them strategically around the room. Then he started moving his hands over your body, never making physical contact. It was as if the two of you engaged in a mystical dance. At times, your body responded to his hands' motions, as if invisible medicine trailed his touch. Throughout the process, he prayed, sang, and made unfamiliar sounds. After about an hour of applying invisible substances to your body, he asked everyone to leave the room except me. He instructed me to remove all your clothing," Mom recounted, her expression filled with profound emotion.

"What happened next?" I asked, my voice brimming with curiosity.

"The strangest thing happened. A boy around your age appeared at our front door. He didn't knock or anything, but the medicine man knew he was there," Mom began.

"Please go to the front door and take the healing bag from Tillzora. I don't want him to come in," the medicine man instructed.

"I went to the door and received the bag from the young boy. He quickly turned and ran off after giving me the bag," Mom continued.

"Their village is 15 miles away," I remarked, with my father and brothers still standing outside my room.

"Yes, I'm aware," Mom acknowledged.

"The bag appeared to be made of three types of animal skin. I carried it to the medicine man, and he opened it. A pungent odor permeated the bedroom and the entire house. He dipped his hand into the bag and retrieved a white, gummy-looking substance, which he proceeded to rub all over your body. After a few minutes, your entire body was covered in this white gum. He asked me to leave the room, and although I didn't want to leave you, I felt it was necessary. Once outside, your dad assured me everything would be fine. Although I had a sense that your dad and the medicine man had met before, neither of them confirmed it. We waited patiently outside the room while he made bizarre noises and chanted for over six hours," Mom recounted.

"I don't remember any of that," I interjected.

"The medicine man continued to chant and sing well past midnight. The pungent smell was so potent that people miles around could detect its funky presence hanging in the air. Everyone in the neighborhood knew what was happening, otherwise, they would have called the police," Mom explained.

"I must have smelled dreadful," I remarked.

"It wasn't until early the next morning that the medicine man decided to leave. He assured me you would be alright. He also gave me some of that smelly medicine and instructed me on how to apply it to your head and chest every two hours. The smell was so repugnant that none of your brothers wanted to apply it initially. But their concern quickly changed their minds, and they took turns applying the medicine," Mom shared.

"The medicine smelled as bad as your old gym socks," Jimmie teased with a smile.

"You smelled like an old, dead skunk," Charles chimed in.

"I disagree; you smelled like an old rotten egg," Roy added.

"Thank you for bringing me back. I couldn't have made it without your love and the medicine man's powerful magic," I expressed, my voice filled with deep emotion.

"One day, you may have to do the same for one of us," Roy remarked.

"I hope not," I replied.

"Baby brother, you always have all the fun. What did you see? Where did you go?" Charles inquired.

For the next 30 minutes or so, I detailed all the experiences I had while wandering through the world of illusions. Eventually, one by one, my family slowly left the room, and I drifted back into dreamless sleep.

With each passing day, my body and mind healed and grew stronger. Soon, I was up and walking again. Over the next few days, I fully recovered and returned to my normal routine. I often thought about the medicine man who had helped me, wanting to meet him and express my gratitude, but ultimately deciding against it.

"I wanted to see the African Medicine Man who helped heal me. One day, I took the bus to the city limits. From there, I walked two miles to the African village. As I entered the village, I looked around. There was not a person in sight -- not a soul.

After a few minutes, a tall man walked toward me. I knew right away that he was the medicine man who had healed me. That funny feeling came over me as I walked toward him.

"Hi, I'm Willie," I said.

"I know. I knew you were coming. That's why all the people are out of sight," he said.

"Where is everyone? Usually the children are out playing," I asked.

"Because Tillzora and I battled for your soul, we must be the first people in the village to greet you. It's out of respect that they remain inside," he explained.

A boy about my age walked toward me in the distance. As he approached, he started singing and performing a dance. He came closer, closer, and closer. When he finally reached us, he continued dancing and singing. While dancing, he circled us nine times.

"This is Tillzora. It was his soul that we used to help you battle the demon," the medicine man said.

"Hi, Tillzora. I thank both of you," I said.

"You're welcome. It required all of our powers to heal you. It was an honor to assist our medicine man," Tillzora said with respect.

Tillzora let out a great yell, and all the people came out of hiding. They started singing as they walked toward me. They sang different songs for about an hour as the medicine man and I talked.

"What kind of spider bit me?" I asked.

"It was not a spider," he answered.

"Was it a bee?"

He looked at me closely, studying my face. I sensed that he was trying to decide if I needed to know.

"Please tell me. What was it?"

"It wasn't just any spider. It was a spider with an evil spirit. The demon was trying to steal your powers and your life. It would have been successful if your spirit had not cried out for help. I felt your plea when it first bit you in the vineyard. I immediately started sending my energy your way, but I needed your mother's alignment and Tillzora's young soul to assist me," he explained.

We talked for another hour before I left the village and walked back to the bus stop. Soon, it came, and I was on my way home. As I sat there looking out of the window, the medicine man's words kept running through my mind.

"It wasn't just a spider. It was a spider with an evil spirit."

Cordova said, "Come back from remembering backwards and be here with me."

"I felt my awareness shift to Cardova; however, I was still very engaged in the experience with the spider. I was back in my body at age eight and fully present with Cardova. I was truly in both places at once and able to quickly view either or both at the same time.

"That is exactly the way Aflathecan and I wanted you to remember that experience. Now, let me tell you the parts that you don't remember.

"I was with Aflathecan in his village, presenting him with a medicine bag made from three different types of animal skin when the spider spirit bit you. We both heard your energetic cry for help and began channeling healing energy to you right away. When your mother came to Aflathecan's village requesting help, we both agreed that it would be best if he stayed in physical form throughout the healing. That provided me with the freedom to operate formless as energy, so I could enter your body and soul.

"Once at your house, Aflathecan began working on you at one level, but I entered your body and traveled with you ethereally. I was with you to help divert you away from following the spider spirit down a path that led to death. When the spirit from the spider energetically pushed you towards sickness or death, I worked hard to move you back on the path to health and healing. For example, when the incredibly large bird was carrying you away, I couldn't stop it, but I could try to direct its path towards healing. That big bird was a death hawk, a form that the negative energy within the spider took to end your life, at least as you knew it to be. All I could do was to try and force it to fly over Thunder Dog's village where they were creating a path of healing energy for you to cross safely back to a world of health, love, and life.

"You remember flying on a gigantic hawk, don't you?" Cardova asked.

Cardova didn't wait for an answer; he just went right on talking.

"I knew Thunder Dog long before you were bitten by the spider. Thunder Dog and I taught each other much about special healing herbs. We even trained with Aflathecan for a time. In fact, the medicine bag that I gave Aflathecan was a gift from Thunder Dog and myself. The bag served two purposes: one was to thank Aflathecan for teaching us about healing herbs, and the second was to give him a useful tool for continuing his healing work. You know how critical a good medicine bag is to a medicine man in helping his people. If the bag is not constructed right, it will rob any herbs placed within it of their powers," Cardova explained.

"So that's what you meant when you said that Thunder Dog was one of your best students," I said.

"There will be plenty of time to talk about Thunder Dog and me. But let's get back to you riding on the back of the death hawk, high in the sky. Since you and I were linked, I directed you to fly over a large Native American tribe and a big herd of buffalo. That tribe was Thunder Dog's, and he was waiting below for us. When we passed over Thunder Dog's village, he and his people sent their healing energy to us."

"How did they do that?" I asked.

"Close your eyes, and let's try remembering together. Let's travel back to the time of remembering. Close your eyes and feel the powerful connection between you and the divine creator. All that has happened is available to you because it resides in space and time forevermore. You can easily access this powerful information. But remember that this past data is dead because the experience is long gone. It can be useful only if you remember that it lives no more; it is only a memory. So just relax, Buffalo Feather, and see what has been unseen and experience it fully," Cardova said.

"What do you see below?" Cardova asked.

"I see a village below with many people, many warriors. They have colorful butterflies, buffaloes, and turtles painted all over their bodies. Some of the people are dancing and singing as they circle a large wooden spider. Others are chanting in some type of healing ceremony. Everyone in the village looks up towards the heavens every few minutes.

Thunder Dog has just placed the wooden spider on the fire. Everyone is throwing sage or dried flowers onto the flaming spider, which is producing a great deal of smoke," I said.

"Thunder Dog and his people are using the smoke from the fire as the vehicle that carries their healing energy to you in the spider's dream world and their prayer request to the Divine Creator. Through ritual, they have transformed fire and smoke from a simple tool into a sacred object used to communicate with the divine creator," Cardova said.

The smoke continued to drift up towards me as I traveled the path of the death hawk.

I felt the energy of the hawk trying to move me out of the path of the oncoming smoke. At the same time, I sensed Cardova's energy forcing me back towards the smoke. For a moment, I was helpless as these two powerful forces played tug-of-war with me. I felt myself moving slowly away from the cloud of healing smoke. It was going to pass right by me. It would come close, but we would just miss it. Cardova was losing.

"I heard a voice say, 'You have the power of the butterfly, buffalo, and the great turtle. Call on their powers to help you. Today is not your time to die.'" Now I know that voice to have been that of Thunder Dog.

I felt my will come alive. I felt a wonderfully strange power flowing through Cardova and myself. It was as if, for the first time, we were acting as one entity, totally aligned to achieve the same purpose: to defeat the evil spider.

Working together, we moved into the healing smoke. Instantly, I heard a long, painful cry come from inside me as the death hawk fought to retain its influence over me.

Slowly, the smoke began to surround me. I heard the singing and chanting of Thunder Dog's people coming through the smoke cloud. I experienced their healing energy so powerfully that it was like having the whole tribe right there with me. Every time the smoke touched me, I felt its healing powers nurturing me and freeing my soul.

Soon, the death hawk had no choice but to leave.

"You didn't have much power, but working together, we were successful. I know it's hard to believe, but it's true. I was with you on much of your journey. Now it's time for you to remember the whole experience. It's filled with rich teachings," Cardova smiled.

Chapter 13

THE STUDENT IS READY

"I don't believe that my intention created this wall of diamonds," I said.

"Go ahead and try something else. We can't move on until you understand your power to create with your thoughts, feelings, and intentions," Cardova said.

"I've heard of yellow diamonds," I said.

Right before my eyes, a few yellow diamonds were intermixed with the white ones. The energy emanating from the wall of white and yellow diamonds was awe-inspiring.

The yellow diamonds began to glow brighter and brighter until a beam of light radiated from them, flowing into the top of my head. I instinctively recognized this as Yang energy. My arms and shoulders relaxed, and I took slow, deep breaths as the universal forces of Yang infused me effortlessly.

A second beam of light formed from the yellow diamonds, descending into the earth beneath me and then flowing up through my legs. Instantly, I recognized this energy as Yin. It moved slowly within and along my thighs, entering the base of my spine and flowing into my lower abdomen, causing my balls to draw up tightly against my belly.

The combination of Yin and Yang energies harmoniously merged within me, creating a sense of balance and alignment. The flow of energy nurtured and revitalized my entire being. I felt a deep connection to the universal forces at play, realizing the immense power I held within to shape my reality.

In this moment of profound realization, I understood the potency of my thoughts, feelings, and intentions. I saw that my consciousness was a canvas upon which I could paint the world I desired. The limitations that had confined me were shattered, replaced by a newfound awareness of my limitless creative potential.

Cardova observed with a knowing smile, acknowledging the transformation taking place within me. He recognized that I had taken a significant step towards embracing my true power and stepping into the realm of conscious creation.

"Now, Buffalo Feather, you begin to understand. Your thoughts, intentions, and beliefs are the brushstrokes that shape your reality. Embrace this newfound understanding and explore the vast possibilities that lie before you," Cardova encouraged, his voice resonating with wisdom.

With a renewed sense of purpose and a heightened awareness of my creative abilities, I gazed at the diamond-adorned walls of my cave. The radiant energies of Yin and Yang intertwined, guiding me towards a deeper connection with the mysteries of the universe and the limitless potential that lay within me.

I tingled all over as the yin and yang energy moved slowly towards each other. I experienced the interplay of these two great universal opposites, which I sensed to be perfectly complementary halves.

Just as I relaxed, seven rays of intense light emanated from the white and yellow diamond wall. Each bright beam concentrated and connected with a different point in my body's energy system. My body jerked as this invisible inter-dimensional cosmic energy ran up and down my energy centers, and I continued to experience the strange tingling sensation.

I felt Cardova's presence within my mind. He was trying to convey a message, but I couldn't make it out. I saw his lips moving, but the words remained unclear. What is he trying to say? I thought, my curiosity piqued.

Amidst the increasing intensity of the energy flowing within me, a sense of concern started to emerge. How do I stop this? Then, I heard Cardova's voice say out loud, "When you're done playing, we can move on."

Realizing that I held the power to shape my reality, I focused my attention on the fire in the pit. Instantly, I felt the energy from the diamonds decrease. Gradually, it dissipated, moving out of my body until it was gone.

"Now, do you understand that you're in control of what you experience and create in this reality and back in your world?" Cardova asked.

"Yes, I am beginning to believe that I create my reality, but my question is, why is it so challenging to maintain that awareness consistently?" I confessed.

"That's a good question. Perhaps this serves as your inquiry for the present. However, the answer to this powerful question is best found within you, wise Buffalo Feather. Why did you make your cave so small? Why do you make your life so small? That is the question I came here to have you ask yourself. Exploring and answering that question will mark the next phase of your journey, and in six months' time, I will return to begin teaching you. You have completed the Journey to Buffalo Feather, and now the student is ready to embark on the Journey to God," Cardova stated.

I slowly opened my eyes, and to my surprise, Cardova was gone. The feather that had been present throughout our encounters had vanished as well. A small white diamond refracted sunlight through the window, serving as a reminder of the profound experiences and lessons I had undergone.

However, in this pivotal moment, I experienced a revelation that dawned upon me. I realized that I stood at the beginning of my training, rather than at the desired end that I had fervently hoped for. The realization brought forth a mix of emotions – a tinge of disappointment, perhaps, but also a profound sense of humility and acceptance.

With this newfound awareness, I recognize that my journey is not a destination but a continuous process of growth and learning. Instead of feeling discouraged, I embrace the understanding that I have merely scratched the surface of my potential. This realization fuels my determination and propels me forward, ready to embrace the challenges and revelations that lie ahead on my path of self-discovery and mastery.

The End.

www.ingramcontent.com/pod-product-compliance
Lightning Source LLC
LaVergne TN
LVHW091534070526
838199LV00001B/52